MARCO POLO

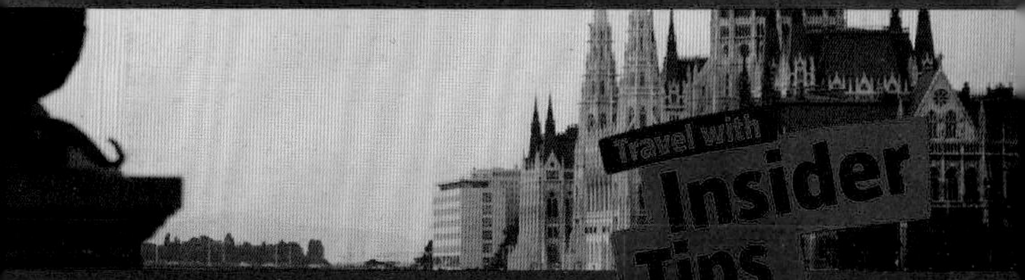

Travel with Insider Tips

BUDAPEST

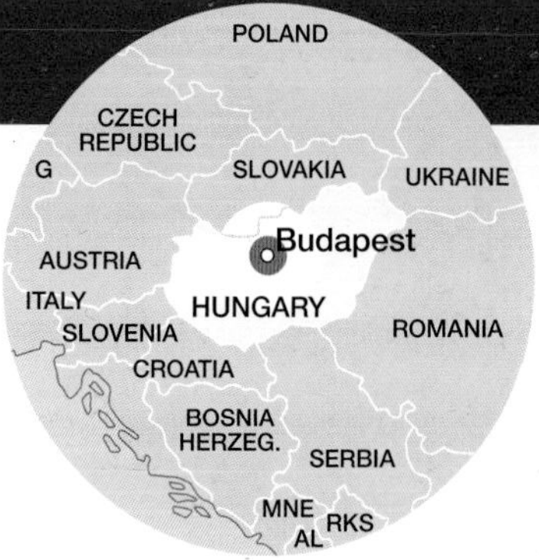
POLAND
CZECH REPUBLIC
G
SLOVAKIA
UKRAINE
Budapest
AUSTRIA
ITALY
HUNGARY
SLOVENIA
ROMANIA
CROATIA
BOSNIA HERZEG.
SERBIA
MNE
RKS
AL

www.marcopolouk.com

1964Th.

914
391
BUD

← INSIDE FRONT COVER:
THE BEST HIGHLIGHTS

The best Insider Tips → p. 4

INSIDER TIP

Best of ... → p. 6

Sightseeing → p. 26

Food & drink → p. 56

SYMBOLS

INSIDER TIP	Insider Tip
★	Highlight
●●●●	Best of ...
🌤	Scenic view
☉	Responsible travel: for ecological or fair trade aspects
(*)	Telephone numbers that are not toll-free

PRICE CATEGORIES HOTELS

Expensive over 40,000 forints

Moderate 27,000–40,000 forints

Budget under 27,000 forints

The prices are for a double room per night including breakfast

PRICE CATEGORIES RESTAURANTS

Expensive 4500 forints

Moderate 3500–4500 forints

Budget under 3500 forints

The prices are based on a main course and a drink

On the cover: Arcades and towers high above the Danube p. 30 | In the old Jewish quarter p. 48

CONTENTS

Shopping → p. 66

Entertainment → p. 74

Where to stay → p. 82

Street atlas → p. 114

DID YOU KNOW?
Relax & enjoy → p. 32
Keep fit! → p. 35
Books & films → p. 39
Sporty & strong → p. 44
Gourmet restaurants → p. 60
Local specialities → p. 62
Luxury hotels → p. 86
Budgeting → p. 103
Currency converter → p. 105
Weather in Budapest → p. 106

MAPS IN THE GUIDEBOOK
(116 A1) Page numbers and co-ordinates refer to the street atlas.
(0) Site/address located off the map.
General map of Budapest and the surrounding area pp. 130/131
An underground / tram map can be found in the inside back cover

INSIDE BACK COVER:
PULL-OUT MAP →

PULL-OUT MAP
(A–B 2–3) Refers to the removable pull-out map

The best MARCO POLO Insider Tips

Our top 15 Insider Tips

INSIDER TIP ▸ Sweet temptation

The Café Auguszt combines tradition and organic ingredients to produce delicious creations. Be it ice cream or cakes: the quality is outstanding and the ambience and bistro-table decor make this a perfect place to sit back and enjoy → **p. 58**

INSIDER TIP ▸ Fabric heaven

Young Hungarian designers have made their dream of a joint project come true with Eventuell Gallery, where they sell their hand-made, very colourful creations. They use mainly fabrics to make a variety of beautiful and useful items → **p. 71**

INSIDER TIP ▸ Ready for the stage

In Merlin's restaurant you can experience the theatre ambience and enjoy fare from Europe or Asia in an artistic setting. On Fridays and Saturdays the parties go on until the early hours and are particularly lively → **p. 62**

INSIDER TIP ▸ Stylish

Arioso, a dream shop selling flowers and decorative goods for the home is a perfect spot to take a break while exploring trendy Király utca and enjoy a cup of coffee - in the cosy courtyard, weather permitting → **p. 71**

INSIDER TIP ▸ Courtly glamour

More and more new spaces can be admired and appreciated in Gozsdu Court, a complex of wonderfully restored apartments in the Jewish Quarter (photo top) → **p. 48**

INSIDER TIP ▸ Fine Arts

Koller Galéria has more than just art to stimulate the senses. The attractive premises in Budapest's Castle District have an unusual flair and an inviting sculpture garden → **p. 68**

INSIDER TIP ▸ Show time

The new Ram Colosseum theatre and event venue is the ideal stage for the rousing dance ensemble Experidance → **p. 81**

INSIDER TIP creative nest

The long-established Fészek (Nest) Artists' Club has become the garden restaurant Flamingo, a Mediterranean oasis serving multicultural cuisine → **p. 61**

INSIDER TIP Stylish comeback

The former Luxus department store, a magnificent Art Nouveau building on Vörösmarty tér, has, after many years, undergone a stylish refurbishment. The new shopping complex is called Váci 1 (photo bottom) → **p. 69**

INSIDER TIP Musical bliss

Whether Gypsy Princess or Merry Widow: moving sounds in front of a great backcloth can be enjoyed during concerts on the operetta ship → **p. 79**

INSIDER TIP Trendy designs

Cool and experimental: in the fashion shop Retrock de Luxe young Hungarian and international fashion designers show off their hip creations → **p. 72**

INSIDER TIP Eco gallery

Fun recycling design in the shop and fair-trade coffee: Printa is a versatile creative community in the Jewish Quarter. The young alternative scene contributes a lot to the new attractiveness of this neighbourhood → **p. 72**

INSIDER TIP colourful

Hip location: the imaginatively designed Csendes Bar is particularly popular with creative types and students → **p. 77**

INSIDER TIP Water bed

Dreaming on the waves of the Danube and breakfasting on the terrace: these pleasant prospects can be enjoyed on the Fortuna floating hotel → **p. 88**

INSIDER TIP Summer in the city

Relaxing, flirting, reading: the small Károlyi kert park is a place of relaxation for children, but also for students and adults. It is an oasis in the busy city → **p. 96**

BEST OF ...

GREAT PLACES FOR FREE
Discover new places and save money

FOR FREE

● *Imposing architectural mix*

EU citizens can visit the *Hungarian Parliament Building* for free. This edifice, completely oversized, but certainly fantastic to look at, says a lot about the state of Hungarian national pride at the time it was built → **p. 38**

● *Island break*

The 2-km long, car-free *Margaret Island* is a leisure space that costs precisely nothing. The green spaces are lovely places to have picnics, while the paths and gardens are perfect for extended walks. Some pretty destinations in the northern part of the island are the water tower, the musical fountain and the Japanese garden → **p. 37**

● *Bastion with a view*

Everyone is captivated by the magnificent view of the city that can be enjoyed for free: the *Fisherman's Bastion* on Castle Hill is an architectural gem and a stage for young and old. Lovers can find nooks to be alone together, while children can explore the walkways and passages (photo right) → **p. 30**

● *Free ride*

All across the capital: pensioners from EU countries can travel for free in Budapest. They can use all public transport without having to buy a ticket → **p. 40**

● *Church in the rock*

The monks ought to charge an entrance fee for this experience: those who take a time out from their sightseeing marathon will find shelter in the *Gellért rock chapel*, an oasis of calm in a small cave, away from all the hustle and bustle → **p. 32**

● *Summertime fireworks*

A great show that everyone can experience for free is the big firework display put on over the citadel on the evening of 20 August, the feast of *St Stephen of Hungary*. On this day the whole of Budapest is transformed into one big party → **p. 99**

● ● ● ● Dots in guidebook refer to 'Best of ...' tips

ONLY IN BUDAPEST
Unique experiences

● *Iconic Bridge*
The best end to a romantic evening, according to the
people of Budapest, is walking home across the
Chain Bridge. And indeed the bridge, which is
lit up at night, is a wonderful spot to take in
the magical atmosphere of a city on the
water (photo left) → **p. 37**

● *Place to be*
When it comes to lifestyle and nightlife,
Liszt Ferenc tér, 'Franz Liszt Square', sets
the tone. Here, not far from the elegant
boulevard Andrássy út, you will find one
hip café next to another. → **p. 44**

● *Incredible Ambience*
The *New York Kávéház* is brilliant! You should see
this café at least once, for it is the most breathtaking
representative of the Budapest café tradition: other cafés may
be cosier, but here visitors can feast their eyes on the overwhelming
décor. → **p. 59**

● *Heroes' Square*
Budapest's skateboarders enjoy themselves under the eyes of Archangel Gabriel on *Heroes' Square.* History has been set in stone here:
from the top of the two columned arches Hungarian rulers and states-
men look down at the hustle and bustle on the city's largest square.
→ **p. 43**

● *The Queen of Desserts*
The name Gundel put Budapest and the whole of Hungary on the culinary map. As a result, Gundel palacsinta, a pancake with walnuts and
chocolate sauce, is both a tasty treat and a piece of cultural heritage.
These pancakes can be tasted in *Centrál Kávéház,* for example. → **p. 58**

● *Remembrance and Experience*
The Moorish-Byzantine onion domes of the *Dohány Street Synagogue*
are the landmark of an urban cosmos that is unique in Europe: a once
again very lively Jewish Quarter. The synagogue is a very handsome
building, but it's also a memorial to all those who suffered and per-
ished during the Holocaust → **p. 49**

ONLY IN

BEST OF ...

● *A villa full of art*
At the *Kogart Gallery* on the elegant Andrássy út you can dine while surrounded by outstanding works of art. The smart villa houses one of the largest private Hungarian collections of contemporary art and its restaurant is a wonderful place to take a break. → **p. 44**

● *Welcome to the opera*
The magnificence of the Renaissance Revival: just a glance into the foyer will convince you that a guided tour through the *State Opera House* is worthwhile. → **p. 45**

● *Delicious fast food*
The *Great Market Hall* sells every conceivable Hungarian culinary delicacy. Don't miss the *langós* stall on the first floor: this is the only place to experience just how tasty a stuffed potato-yeast flatbread can be (photo) → **p. 64**

● *Old Masters*
The *Museum of Fine Arts* is Budapest's most magnificent temple of European art. Among the highlights are the Old Masters on the first floor. The Spanish collection with works by El Greco and Goya is particularly impressive. → **p. 45**

● *In memoriam*
The *Holocaust Memorial Centre* has such dignity and beauty that visiting it will be an unforgettable experience. Walking through the building is an incredibly haunting experience, ending in the wonderfully restored Páva Synagogue → **p. 50**

● *Going underground*
The *Buda Castle Labyrinth* provides insights into the city's underworld. The dimly lit caves are peppered with historical and mystical depictions. → **p. 29**

RAIN

RELAX AND CHILL OUT
Take it easy and spoil yourself

● *Wellness from head to toe*

A city tour leaves you full of impressions and is often quite exhausting. You can switch off and pamper yourself with ayurvedic massages, facials and body treatments in the *Mandala Day Spa*. → **p. 32**

● *A café with style*

The café of the *Gresham Palace* Hotel is a feast for the eyes. Walk through the main entrance to the reception and then turn right and you'll discover not just some outstanding Art Nouveau décor, but that even the cakes are small works of art. → **p. 86**

● *Sounds for the soul*

The Budapest Klezmer Band is a leading exponent of a kind of music that is conquering ever larger audiences, in clubs and at the annual *Jewish Summer Festival* for example. The rousing mix of melancholy and jolly sounds is a wonderful treat for the soul. → **p. 99**

● *Bathing pleasures*

The *Széchenyi Thermal Baths* in the City Park is an architectural oasis of luxury. With their warm water the open-air thermal pools are a pleasure in any weather. → **p. 46**

● *Romantic dinners*

When the setting sun bathes the city and the river in a magical light, the guests on the *Spoon* restaurant boat are in an enviable spot to enjoy the atmosphere. There is hardly a more relaxing way to end a day, because in addition to the good view the food is also excellent (photo) → **p. 61**

● *Classical sounds*

The *Béla Bartók Concert Hall* is part of the Palace of Arts. This hi-tech hall has excellent acoustics. Come here to enjoy concerts by the Hungarian National Philharmonic Orchestra and performances by orchestras and soloists from around the world. → **p. 78**

INTRODUCTION

DISCOVER BUDAPEST!

What a panorama! The view from the Fisherman's Bastion over the Danube, its bridges and the Hungarian capital is stunning. The setting alone is unique: The Buda district is situated on the elevations of the Buda Hills; opposite it, on the other side of the Danube, is the flat Pest. Both riverbanks are lined by beautiful architecture: on the Pest side is the Hungarian Parliament Building and many magnificent townhouses, on the Buda side is the formidable Buda Castle and Gellért Hill with its Citadel. Ten bridges span the Danube and they contribute much to the capital's charm.

Even a good 20 years after the fall of Communism in Hungary, Budapest is still a city in the midst of change. It is striving for authenticity, modernity and a higher quality of life. The city looks more glamorous every year. One example of this urban development is the 'New City Centre' project, which includes an enormous, post-modern glass structure complete with zeppelin-shaped roof in Bécsi utca, near Vörösmarty tér. Four old buildings have had to be demolished to make way for this futuristic

Photo: Danube with the Chain Bridge

complex; from 2013 visitors will be able to admire views of the Danube from its park-like roof terrace.

Budapest is the head, heart and soul of the country

The capital is home to 1.7 million people. This figure alone speaks volumes about its significance. Debrecen, Hungary's second-largest city, has a population of only 207,000. Some 17 percent of all of Hungary's citizens live in Budapest. Budapest is the symbol of Hungarian national pride; it is the head, heart and soul of the country, and this is what makes living here so special.

Take Ilona as an example: the 33-year-old banker has managed the leap from rural Hungary to the capital. She has a net monthly income of 200,000 forints (about 600 pounds / 900 US-dollars), which is above average. She also owns her own home. Home-ownership is everything to the people of Budapest, and Hungary in general. Ilona's flat is tiny, yet her mortgage and associated expenses take up more than half of her earnings. From what she has left there is no way she can afford to own and run a car. She takes the bus and train to work. That is another thing Ilona has in common with most other people in Budapest. Public transport is the most important means of transport and during rush hour the trains and buses are packed.

Architectural gem and Budapest's landmark: Buda Castle

Budapest has the highest wages in the country. Yet it is almost impossible for most people to get rich from working. The cost of living is as high as in Western countries; as a result wages only allow for a modest existence. Everyday life is tough for most people in Budapest. Nevertheless they are their city's biggest fans. That is because Budapest is where the action is: the markets have goods that can only be found in Budapest, international music stars only perform in the capital and it is only here that cinema blockbusters are released and major sporting events and festivals are held.

During the summer months Budapest is a veritable open-air Mecca. The banks of the Danube and Margaret Island, the City Park, other parks and

> **During the summer the city is a complete open-air Mecca**

the Buda Hills are all places the people of Budapest like to flock to every free minute they get. They go out and they go out. That is also true of families: Lájos, Lydia and their two children live in one of the prefab high-rise apartment blocks on the Buda side of the city. They have a tight budget, but there's no penny-pinching when it comes to quality time with their children. The zoo, the circus, the children's railway, rollerblading on Margaret Island, trips to the shopping centre and the Buda Hills are all things this family enjoys, making Budapest a colourful place for them to live.

Going out for meals is also as vital to the people of Budapest as the air they breathe, despite not having much money. The many inexpensive restaurants are the preferred destinations. Although there is much room for improvement when it comes to service and cleanliness, they are popular meeting places. You can spend hours having a good time and enjoying Hungarian fare here. Young people fancy McDonald's and Burger King, but most young people in Budapest are far more involved in family life than their counterparts in Western countries. Eating together as a family is something of a ritual.

Mártha is a representative of the older generation: she was born in Budapest and has remained loyal to the city her whole life. For the 83-year-old a cup of coffee in the Astoria Hotel is absolute luxury. Meeting up with her friends there is a must, she says, even though her monthly pension of 80,000 forints is not really enough to justify it. Among her other pleasures are visits to the thermal baths. Pensioners can use the city's public transport for free, which makes her mobile. The therapeutic treatments are paid for by her health insurance. Budapest's thermal baths are more than just spas for the older people; they are places to enjoy and to meet people.

The people of Budapest are well practised in making the best of things. And there is one thing in particular that they all have in common: they are proud to be from capital, blessed with the unshakable self-confidence that comes from knowing that they set the pace and the tone. They may spend the week in the city, but during the summer months at least, the exodus begins on Fridays. The most popular destinations are the nearby Lake Velence, Lake Balaton and the Danube Bend. Among the people who like to escape the city will be those who managed to acquire a little holiday getaway during the country's Communist years, or those visiting friends and relatives. Alternatively, they may be travelling with holiday vouchers, a form of holiday pay issued by companies. The people of Budapest are city people of a somewhat different, typically Hungarian kind. The 'we' is more important than the 'I', and families are hugely important. Family members stick together, celebrate birthdays, Easter and Christmas together and are the most important source of support in times of need. Social relationships define everyday life at every age: students find friends for life in their halls of residence; they celebrate and cook together. Expensive cinema and nightclub visits are the exception, but they still know how to have lots of fun.

History is omnipresent in the minds of Budapest's inhabitants

On the Feast of St Stephen of Hungary, the most important national holiday, celebrated on 20 August, hundreds of thousands of people from Budapest take to the streets, squares and bridges. History is omnipresent in the minds of everyone in Budapest. It all began in 896 with the 'land seizure' of the seven Magyar tribes under the leadership of Grand Prince Árpád. The first King of Hungary, Stephen I, whose coronation took place in AD1000, is especially revered. The Holy Crown of Hungary is also known as the Crown of St Stephen, and it is on permanent display in the central domed hall of the Hungarian Parliament Building in Budapest. After the Mongols overran the country in 1241–2, Béla IV of Hungary built the first fortress on Castle Hill. Matthias Corvinus, King of Hungary from 1458–90, had it extended in the Renaissance style. This Golden Age was followed by 160 years of continuous occupation by the Turks (1526–1668). By the time the battle against the occupying power was successfully won, Buda and Pest were completely destroyed.

In 1941, Hungary took Germany's side in World War II against the Soviet Union. During the Nazi reign of terror, supported by the Hungarian Arrow Cross Party, Budapest's Jewish Quarter was turned into a ghetto and a graveyard for thousands. At the end of the war large areas of the city lay in ruins. In 1947 the Communist Party came to power. Protests by students in Budapest triggered resistance against the regime in 1956, but the revolt of the 'counter-revolutionaries' was brutally suppressed. Decades later in the night leading up to 11 September 1989, Hungary opened its borders, allowing around 100,000 East German citizens, including many who had been put up in a camp in Budapest, to escape. On 23 October, on the 33rd anniversary of the Revolution of 1956, the Republic of Hungary was proclaimed from a window of the Hungarian Parliament Building. That marked the end of the Communist People's Republic.

For the past 20 years or so, the spotlight in Budapest has been focused mainly on the flourishing cityscapes: the wonderfully restored beacons of historic Budapest, the huge international investment in shopping centres and luxury real estate, and on large projects such as the Millennium Quarter around Lagymányosi Bridge. The darker sides of progress have tended to be ignored, however. The most recent economic crisis has increased public-sector financial problems as well as social tensions.

Even in liberal Budapest, the word 'international' does not have a good ring to it anymore. It stands for the international corporations who are to blame for the huge rises in utility bills, and for the banks to whom many homeowners are in debt and are at risk of losing the roof over their head, and it stands for the many fraud scandals associated with the privatisation of once-public companies. As the country's political and economic centre, Budapest is a kind of lens that concentrates all these problems.

A very special kind of city-on-the-river magic

People are taking stock in the capital. The most important question is: in what way have the past 20 years benefited 'ordinary' Hungarians? Budapest is focusing more than ever on the difficult living conditions of the majority and on the city's unique

A welcome refreshment after a shopping spree in Váci utca

Hungarian identity. The people of the city want the Budapest of tomorrow to be different. What should it look like? The answer is not yet clear.

The beauty of the city remains untouched by all of that. When the floodlights bathe the sights on the Danube in a beautiful light every evening, nobody is left untouched by their spell. Visitors to Budapest will find a very special kind of 'city-on-the-river' magic, a city that is more than the sum of its sunny sides.

1 Get moving

Dance Modern dance is really popular in the city on the Danube, for example on the stage of the Trafó House of Contemporary Arts *Trafó Kortárs Művészetek Háza; Liliom utca 41, www.trafo.hu, photo)*. You can enjoy Hungarian folk music and attend dance nights at the *Fonó Budai Zeneház* entertainment complex *(Sztregova utca 3, www.fono.hu)*. The annual dance festival Szóló Duó, which gets the whole city dancing every January, is an absolute must *(www.szoloduo.com)*.

Re-fashion

2

Original new uses It doesn't always have to be brand new! Glasses made of old vinyl and filmstrips are available from *Orange Optica (Király utca 38, www.tipton.hu)*. The eco-designers at *Konkrét Labor* create fabulous fashion, home accessories and art objects from discarded materials *(konkretlabor. blogspot.com, photo)*, while Karton Design just outside the city produces furniture from cardboard *(Szent István utca 102, Törökbálint, www.kartondesign.com)*. The landscape architecture group *Tájék Tájművészeti* transforms scrap metal into flower sculptures *(www.tajek.hu)*.

3 Decorative

Individual and hand-made The people of Budapest have a penchant for wearing unusual accessories. Very popular are the jewellery artworks by the goldsmith *Márta Edőcs (www.martaedocs.hu)* and the unusual designs by *Fanni Király (www.kiralyfanni.com, photo)*. *Regina Kaintz* often uses barbed wire in her pieces, in combination with gemstones *(www. reginakaintz.com)*. The leading showcase for small-scale jewellery designers is *Magma Galerie (Petőfi Sándor utca 11, www.magma.hu)*.

Architecture

Eye-catching buildings Budapest is known for its neoclassical and Gothic churches. A guided tour with *Human Design (Hollan Ernö utca 49, www.human-design.net)* will give you a good introduction to the city's architecture. As part of their city tour they visit the Papp-Laszlo-Arena, the Palace of Arts and interesting office buildings such as the ING head-quarters on Dózsa György utca and the ensemble at Eiffel tér *(photo)*. The Farkasréti cemetery (Farkasréti temető) is worth visiting not just because it is where Béla Bartók is buried, but also for its funeral chapel by Imre Makovecz whose interior is designed to look like a human ribcage, the wooden trusses on the ceiling being the ribs. The *CET Budapest* between Petőfi Bridge and Liberty Bridge has given culture a new home and is also eye-catching because of its abstract form *(www.cet-budapest.hu)*.

Dual use

Party in a pool & rock in a school Things can get quite lively in the city's thermal baths. Several times a month they host electronic music parties, and are great places to have fun *(www.cinetrip.hu)*. The old *Millénáris* factory is also being put to new uses. The industrial venue hosts concerts and art exhibitions *(Kis Rókus utca 16–20, www.millenaris.hu)*. Culture is also the order of the day in a unique heritage school building. The programme in the 5300 sq m *Tűzraktér* is extensive, ranging from dance, music and performance art to photography and fashion *(Hegedű utca 3, www.tuzrakter.hu)*.

IN A NUTSHELL

ART NOUVEAU

Budapest is defined by a diverse mix of architectural styles, of which Hungarian Art Nouveau really stands out. It was primarily shaped by the architect Ödön Lechner (1845–1914). Lechner used Hungarian folk art as well as the Indian and Persian formal vocabulary to create a fascinating architectural style with curving lines and animal and floral ornaments. The Zsolnay factory, where colourful majolica was made, played a key role. Its products adorn the dome of the Museum of Applied Arts, the most magnificent structure that Lechner and his colleague Guyla Pártos (1845 – 1916) created. Most Art Nouveau buildings are to be found in the city centre (Belváros und Lipótváros) and near the City Park.

They include the Gresham Palace hotel on Széchenyi István tér (formerly Roosevelt tér), the Post Office Savings Bank building (Magyar Király Takarék Pénztár) in Hold utca and Thonet Ház in Váci utca 11. An Art Nouveau gem in Budapest's Zoo is the elephant house. Near the City Park on Városligeti fasor you can find the Art Nouveau villas Eger (no. 24) and Vidor (no. 33).

BACKYARD SCENE

Easy going à la Budapest takes place in backyards during the summer months. The top address among backyard bars is Szimpla kert. Like several others, this one is well established, but others just exist for a single summer. Whose backyard will be turned into a bar next? The only

Photo: The Art Nouveau Elephant House in Budapest's zoo

More than just tradition: Budapest stands for the Danube and thermal baths, and for a country undergoing radical economic change

way to find out is to listen to the rumours. New cult venues open up every summer. One thing all the backyard bars have in common is their cool ambience, accompanied by varying degrees of appealing dereliction. The seating is outdoors, the scene is young, casual and often interested in art. The prices tend to range from average to inexpensive.

COFFEE HOUSE TRADITION

Coffee houses – classic cafés with great ambience – are a wonderful part of Budapest tradition. Towards the end of the 19th century and the beginning of the 20th, they were the meeting places of the country's elite: authors and painters, intellectuals and journalists. World War II marked the end for the *kávéház* culture. However, since the fall of Communism in 1989, the tradition has been flourishing again. The grand old names such as New York, Central, Művész and Gresham are back with renewed glamour.

ENVIRONMENTAL AWARENESS

There are said to be more than 20,000 scrap cars on the streets of Budapest. The people of this city are used to smog alarm, both in summer and in winter, but the state and its citizens have one thing in common: in reality they pay little attention to protecting their environment. Legal requirements such as emission controls are enforced only half-heartedly. That suits many people because it is cheaper. Although EU regulations are passed into national law, there are often worlds between what is written on paper and what happens in reality. Green policies are lacking in Budapest as are environmental awareness and urban green spaces. Only 2.4 percent of Budapest's area is green space (by contrast 30 percent of London is made up open green space and park land). Nice green spaces for children to play are particularly hard to find.

HOLY CROWN

The Crown of St Stephen, the Holy Crown of Hungary, has the status of national relic and features on the Hungarian coat of arms. Stephen (997 – 1038) was the first king of Hungary, but he never wore the crown that is now on display in the Hungarian Parliament. It is not known exactly when the 2.5 kg exhibition piece was made. After World War II the crown found its way to the United States, but was returned to Hungary in 1978 at the behest of President Carter. As part of an act of state, the crown was moved to the Hungarian Parliament Building on 1 January 2000, an event watched by thousands. The Holy Crown of Hungary has increasingly become a symbol of national unity and greatness as well as of the Hungarians' Christian-Magyar identity. Stephen, who used all means possible to convert Hungary to Catholicism, also went down in the Hungarian Constitution in 2011 as the official founder of the state.

JAZZ MEETS BLUES & KLEZMER

Jazz, pop, soul: Kati Rácz is a star in the jazz scene with a powerful voice and her fans adore her. Together, she and her band are called *Kati Rácz és a Flush*. Budapest's hip clubs scramble to get artists like her. 'My music,' says Kati Rácz, 'is urban, or rather: Budapesty'. Through their roots, artists like Kati Rácz and Ferenc Jávori, the leader of the Budapest Klezmer Band, also incorporate a Budapest element into their music. Kati Rácz has a Roma father and a Jewish mother. Roma roots, Jewish roots: that's something Rácz has in common with many artists in this scene. These roots generate a sound that is exciting to listen to, because it draws on all kinds of different traditions. The Budapest Klezmer Band has set standards in a special way. Jávori calls his music a blend of traditional Jewish Klezmer, Latin rhythms and jazz, the 'blues of the 21st century'. The jazz and Klezmer scene in Budapest is alive and well. Don't miss it!

LANGUAGE

Hungary's insular character is most clearly expressed in its language, which is not comparable to any other. It is a member of the Finno-Ugric language group, but only specialists in historical linguistics can discern the features it has in common with Finnish.

Visitors to Budapest will do just fine with English and German. It is, however, difficult to communicate in public authorities and on local transport. It is important to know that names are written in reverse order: the surname is listed first, then the 'first' name. This is also true for dates: first comes the year, then the month and then the day.

MAGICAL CAVES

On the hilly Buda side of the Danube, the city possesses a unique 'underworld'. The enormous labyrinthine caves of Budapest are hydrothermal caves that were formed by the same springs that today supply the thermal baths, washing out countless passages and halls from the limestone and creating beautiful formations.

Four cave areas are open to the public: the most accessible cave system for tourists is the Labyrinth of Buda Castle in District I. The latest attraction, the Hospital in the Rock, is also in the Castle district, near Matthias Church. Northwest of Margaret Bridge in District II there are two caves open to the public that have fascinating stalactites and other mineral formations: the Pálvölgyi and Szemlöhegyi caves.

From time to time new caves come to light deep under Budapest. In 2008, scientists presented their most recent find: a 25-m (82ft) high dome-shaped room. In 2003, a group of scientists discovered a lake with a depth of almost 54m (177ft) and filled with 300,000 litres of thermal water. It is Hungary's deepest body of water.

Budapest's coffee house tradition in all its glory: the New York

MUSICAL TITANS

Hungary's classical music composers are omnipresent in Budapest. First and foremost there is Ferenc (Franz) Liszt (1811–86). In 1875 Liszt became the first president of Budapest's Academy of Music. The Austrian Compromise of 1867 resulted in a surge of national self-confidence and pride, and this had a massive impact on the country's musical masters, who began to go in search of their musical roots. Thus, Liszt introduced a class for the study of Hungarian folk songs at the Academy.

Two musical geniuses were particularly passionate about folk songs: they were Béla Bartók (1881–1945) and Zoltán Kodály (1882–1967). From 1906 both of them travelled extensively, writing down ancient Hungarian songs. The melodies flowed into the masters' compositions, contributing to their uniqueness and making a lasting tribute to the tradition of Magyar song. On Andrássy út 89, where Zoltán Kodály lived from 1924 until his death, there is a Kodaly Memorial Museum (Kodály Zoltán Emelékmuzeum és Archivum). Béla Bartók lived in a villa in the Buda Hills at Csalán út 29. It is now the Bela Bartók Memorial House (Bartók Béla Emlékhaz).

NATIONALISM

The majestic Turul statue towers high up on Budapest's Castle Hill. This mythical Hungarian creature, a mix of falcon and eagle, provides good material for lovely stories, but it has also been co-opted for extreme right-wing interpretations of history and racist agendas. In the 1940s it became the symbol of the Hungarian fascists, the Arrow Cross Party. Today, Hungary's ring-wing extremists come together in the Jobbik party, which won almost 17 percent of the vote in the 2010 parliamentary elections. The red and white Árpád flag of the first Hungarian dynasty is also being used by the right for its own purposes and is part of a spooky Trianon cult. The 1920 Treaty of Trianon (one of the palaces in Versailles), formally ended World War I as fought between Hungary and the victorious allies; Hungary lost two-thirds of its territory and 3.2 million citizens to neighbouring countries. Using the Turul, the Árpád flag and the reference to Trianon, the cult invokes a Hungary of its former size and a Magyar nation that goes beyond the present borders. Nationalism also determines the policies of the Fidesz party, which came to power in 2010. One of the first things it did was to introduce an annual Trianon commemoration in parliament.

READY WIT

The secret weapon of the people of

The Szechényi Baths: combining architectural grandeur and pool fun

Budapest is their wit. Urgin Aranka and Vargha Kálman write about it in the anthology 'Budapest Cocktail': 'As Gemütlichkeit goes with the people from Vienna, so wit goes with the people of Budapest.' The people of this city always have a joke at hand to keep themselves going in every situation life throws at them, never mind how hopeless it is. They only admit defeat when they can no longer think of a joke. And that is a day many people who do not live in the city wait for, because although the people of Budapest are admired for their cleverness, they are also considered arrogant and snobbish. And so if they had to admit defeat, there would be no shortage of secret schadenfreude.

SINTI AND ROMA

János Bihari (1764–1825) was known as the 'gypsy king'. The violinist was a Romany, a member of the Roma people. He became a star in the 18th century and played with his band in Budapest's most elegant restaurants. Franz Liszt was one of his biggest fans. Other violin virtuosos followed in János Bihari's footsteps and achieved fame and recognition with their orchestras. Today, there are hardly any restaurants left that still employ a Roma band, and talk of the extinction of a cultural institution is justified.

The Sinti and Roma are struggling more than ever in Hungary. Discrimination and exclusion are widespread, and the unemployment rate is high. Many Sinti and Roma people live in Budapest's eastern District XIII (Józsefváros). That is also the location of the Roma parliament, an action group with social workers, a community centre and an art exhibition. The poverty is evident.

THE DANUBE

The Danube has a wealth of experiences to offer visitors to the city. You could, for example, arrive by hydrofoil from Vienna or as part of a river cruise, go on a boat trip to the Danube Bend or book a sightseeing tour. If you want to go out, you could dine on a boat restaurant, enjoy an onboard jazz concert or dance to DJ music on a ship's deck on warm summer nights.

For the national holiday on 20 August, the day of St Stephen of Hungary, people fight to get their hands on boat tickets in order to watch the firework display over the city from the water. Only those who book very early will be lucky enough to get tickets.

THERMAL BATHS AND SPAS

Budapest has twelve thermal baths, making it an attractive spa town. Whether they are used for healing purposes or for fun, going to one of the baths is part of the local way of life. The baths' architecture has everything to offer, from the Turkish period to the present. The architectural highlights include the Turkish Rác Baths, the stylish Rudas Baths, the neo-Baroque splendour of Széchenyi Baths and the Art Nouveau magnificence of the Gellért Baths.

TRAFFIC CHAOS

Careful drivers will have a tough time in Budapest. Most drivers here tend to put their foot down and only brake when they have to. The many traffic jams and the condition of many of the roads do not make travelling by car in Budapest an appealing prospect. There are also far too few multi-storey and underground car parks. If you want to spare your nerves and not waste any time, you will be better off using the quite good public transport options.

THE PERFECT DAY
Budapest in 24 hours

09:00am UP FISHERMAN'S BASTION

The best way to get into the mood for Budapest is by taking a trip in the historic cable car (Sikló) from Clark Ádám tér near Chain Bridge up to Castle Hill. The panorama gets more magnificent with every metre the cable car ascends. The trip ends outside the mighty *Buda Castle* → p. 29. To the north of the cable car is Szentháromság tér where the *Fisherman's Bastion* → p. 30 (photo left) is located. Climbing up this romantic fortress is a must, because the views from the top are outstanding, with the Danube and the whole of Pest at your feet.

10:00am CHURCH OF OUR LADY (MATTHIAS CHURCH) & OLD STREETS

Also situated on Szentháromság tér is *Matthias Church* → p. 33, a colourful feast for the eyes both inside and out. It was here that the Renaissance king Matthias Corvinus celebrated both of his weddings. When strolling along the surrounding streets, you will find a picturesque, medieval ambience. The bistro restaurant *Café Pierrot* → p. 60 near Szentharomság tér is a good place to take a break after a walk through the city.

11:30am ARCHITECTURAL KALEIDOSCOPE

Take bus number 16 (Burgbus/Várbusz) from Szentharomság tér to Széll Kálmán tér (previously Moszkva tér) and from there the underground line number 2 to Kossuth Lajos tér by the *Parliament Building* → p. 38. A walk through the streets will sum up the meaning of the term 'eclecticism' beautifully: the different architectural styles come together to produce a visual treat. On the way to Szabadság tér (through Báthory utca) in Honvéd utca 3 is Bedő ház with its outstanding Art Nouveau façade. Time for lunch? At the northeastern corner of Szabadság tér is the wonderfully restored Art Nouveau café *Szabadság* → p. 59. Around the corner, in Hold utca, you will be confronted with a masterpiece designed by the architect Ödön Lechner: the former Post Office Savings Bank (Magyar Király Takarék Pénztár), which is now the National Bank.

01:00pm STROLL TO THE BASILICA

Hercegprimás utca runs southwards to *St Stephen's Basilica* → p. 39. Stop for a moment at the lower end of Szent István tér: the view of the neoclassical basilica with its enormous dome is almost as beautiful as the church's interior.

Discover Budapest at its best: in the thick of things, relaxed – and all in a single day

`02:00pm` UNDERGROUND LINE 1 TO HEROES' SQUARE

Near the basilica you will find Bajcsy Zsilinszky út station, which is part of the historic underground line no. 1 (Földalatti). This line is an ideal way to explore the avenue *Andrássy út* → p. 41 (photo bottom left). On *Heroes' Square* → p. 43, where you will also find the Millennium Memorial, you will be right in the midst of Hungarian history. This place also has some great art to offer in the *Museum of Fine Arts* → p. 45 and in the *Hall of Art* → p. 44.

`03:30pm` OFF TO THE CITY PARK

If you feel in the mood, why not take the underground line no. 1 one station further to the *City Park* → p. 45 with its many attractions, and have a look around there. And if you're tired let your mind wander for a while in the palatial *Széchenyi Thermal Baths* → p. 46.

`05:00pm` AROUND THE OPERA HOUSE

Take the underground line no. 1 back to the Opéra station. The *Opera House* → p. 45 is magnificent, but the surrounding buildings on this, the grandest part of Andrássy út, are also impressive. Every business here, be it a shop or a restaurant, is housed in a glorious building, not least the former Paris department store (Parisi Aruház), an Art-Nouveau ensemble dating back to 1911, which now houses the city's best bookshop *Alexandra Könyv és bor* → p. 69. You can get a bite to eat in the smart *Ring Café* → p. 59, which also serves good plats du jour.

`08:00pm` GETTING INTO THE EVENING MOOD

Good Hungarian food and good Hungarian wine: this great start to the evening is available in the restaurant *Bock Bisztro* → p. 60, which belongs to one of the country's top winegrowers. As an alternative try the club and restaurant on board the boat *A38* → p. 80 (photo top). You could also enjoy a drink in the favourite bar of Budapest's creative set, *Csendes Bar* → p. 77 not far from the Hungarian National Museum.

Transport to starting-point:
historic cable-car (Sikló)
Station: Buda Castle
It's best to buy a day ticket for the public transport system.

SIGHTSEEING

WHERE TO START?
Vörösmarty tér (116 C2) *(🕮 D9)*: Vörösmarty Square is an ideal starting point for exploring the city. The magnificent building on the front side houses the legendary Café Gerbeaud. A highlight to the north of the square is St Stephen's Basilica, while the shopping street Váci utca can be found to the south. The panorama from the nearby Vigadó tér/Danube Embankment is stunning: the views across the river extend from Gellért Hill along Castle Hill all the way to the Chain Bridge. Vörösmarty tér is served by underground 1 (Földalatti).

The city of Budapest owes its special character to its late rise to city status in the mid-19th century. The imposing size of many of its buildings was an expression of the optimism the time and the newly-awakening, intense national consciousness.

The only really old building ensemble in the capital is the medieval quarter on Castle Hill. Everywhere else Budapest is a child of the 19th and 20th centuries. Almost everything giving the city its unmistakable character was built during the boom years of 1867 to 1914, the period following the Austro-Hungarian Compromise. The planners incorporated a whole variety of architectural styles in their schemes, from Gothic to Renaissance, neoclassicism and more, including some fine examples of Art Nouveau. The

Photo: Matthias Church

Churches, synagogues and palaces: the enormous diversity of architectural styles in Budapest has become a style in itself

resultant mix made the city the epitome of architectural eclecticism.

Thanks to its situation, Budapest is easy for tourists to get their head around. The busy traffic betrays the fact that the city's political, economic and cultural heart beats in flat Pest, on the eastern banks of the Danube. By comparison, Buda, on the opposite side of the river, is positively tranquil. Large parts of the Castle Quarter with its cobbled streets have a museum-like quality about them. The entire district can be explored on foot. To the north of the Castle Quarter and further south, around Gellért Hill, there are smart residential neighbourhoods. Excavations in Óbuda, north of Buda, have revealed evidence of the Roman presence here. Only little remains of 19th-century Óbuda: the historic buildings had to make way for extensive concrete high-rises after World War II. Those who want to be at the heart of things in Budapest should choose accommodation in the districts close to the Danube in Pest and go on trips to the picturesque world of the Castle Hill from there.

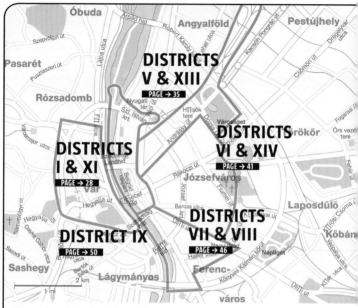

The map shows the location of the most interesting districts. There is a detailed map of each district on which each of the sights described is numbered.

DISTRICTS I & XI

Districts I (Budavár) and XI (Újbuda) are situated on the right bank of the Danube and they also include the Buda Hills, one of the city's preferred residential and recreational areas.

Visitors particularly enjoy exploring the sites close to the Danube, first and foremost the Castle Quarter. Of District I's 26,700 inhabitants, 2,500 live in the alleys of the Castle Quarter.

The Castle Hill ensemble is a fascinating mix. You will find parts of the Baroque town that developed in the 17th century, traces of the medieval town and a lot of showy architecture from the 19th century. Towards the Danube, the most impressive area is between Buda Castle and Matthias Church.

The underground world of Castle Hill is also quite striking. A vast system of passageways extends deep into the hill for several kilometres. A small proportion of them, constituting the Castle Hill Labyrinth, are open to the public.

The Castle Quarter's southern neighbour is Gellért Hill in District XI (population: 136,600) with the Citadel and the imposing Liberty Statue. As is demonstrated by its highly symbolic monuments, not to mention the outstanding architecture of the Gellért Hotel (once the city's most sought-after hostelry), the section of District XI close to the city centre is one of the

SIGHTSEEING

■1 BUDA CASTLE LABYRINTH (BUDAVÁRI LABIRINTUS) ●
(118 B2) (*A8*)

This 1,200-m labyrinth, 16m (50ft) below ground, is a unique attraction. During the day you can explore the 'Prehistoric Labyrinth', the 'Historic Labyrinth' and the 'Labyrinth of Another World'; in the evenings the lights are switched off and visitors only have lanterns to find their way through the maze of passages and halls (6pm–7.30pm), their light creating an almost mythical atmosphere. Exhibits on show include reproductions of cave drawings, Stone-Age hunters and the oversized head of a king wearing a crown. *Daily 9.30am–6pm | I, Úri utca 9 | www.labirintus.com | bus 16 (castle bus/Várbusz)*

■2 BUDA CASTLE (BUDAVÁRI PALOTA)
★ ☆ (119 D–E5) (*B9–10*)

The Castle Quarter, the location of Buda Castle, is around 1000m long and lies 180m (590ft) above sea level. Buda Castle, the city's monumental landmark, was destroyed three times between the 13th and 20th centuries, but always rebuilt. The first castle was commissioned by King Béla IV in the 13th century after the Mongol invasion. This was developed and expanded over the centuries, but then almost completely destroyed during the Great Siege of 1686. A large palace was built on the site in the 18th century under Maria Theresa (1740–80). It was subsequently destroyed two more times: firstly during the Hungarian Revolution of 1848 and then as a result of the siege of 1944–5. After both battles the castle was rebuilt: between 1875 and 1904 it more than doubled in size and was given its striking central dome; during the post-war reconstruction, which lasted into the 1980s, valuable parts of the medieval

MARCO POLO HIGHLIGHTS

royal palace were uncovered. Buda Castle now houses the Hungarian National Gallery, the History Museum and the National Széchenyi Library. Drivers need to purchase special tickets on the roads leading to Castle Hill (there is only a limited number of parking spaces!). If you're on foot the best approach is from Clark Ádám tér via Hunyadi János út. *I., Szent György tér | cable car from Clark Ádám tér, bus 16 (castle bus/Várbusz)*

3 INSIDERTIP HOSPITAL IN THE ROCK (SZIKLAKÓRHÁZ) (118 C3) (*∅ B9*)

This place provides an intriguing glimpse of Budapest's underground world and of

Eye-catching: Fisherman's Bastion

recent Hungarian history. You will learn all about what was long a state secret known only by the code name *LOSK 0101/1*: a military hospital with an operating theatre and the government's nuclear bunker. The caves were used during World War II by the Nazis, and during the Hungarian Revolution of 1956. The nuclear bunker, which was kept in constant operation, is a relic of the Cold War. The entrance is located close to Matthias Church near the castle wall. *Hourly guided tours Tue–Sun 10am–7pm (hospital 30 mins, whole tour 60 mins.) | I, Lovas út 4/c | www.sziklakorhaz.hu | bus 16 (castle bus/Várbusz)*

4 FISHERMAN'S BASTION (HALÁSZBÁSTYA) ★ ⚓ ●
(118 C2–3) (*∅ B8*)

Situated high up above the Danube on Castle Hill, this famous terrace enjoys the best view of the city. The neo-romanesque complex with its walkways, archways and towers, was built at the end of the 19th century, based on designs by the architect Frigyes Schulek (1841–1919), who also remodelled the neighbouring Matthias Church. The name 'Fisherman's Bastion' is a reminder of the fact that there were once defensive walls here that were secured and defended by the guild of fishermen. *I, Szentháromság tér | bus 16 (castle bus/Várbusz)*

5 LIBERTY STATUE (SZABADSÁG SZOBOR) (116 C5) (*∅ C11*)

Standing atop a 26-m (83ft) pedestal, the imposing 14-m (46ft) Liberty Statue on Gellért Hill, of a woman holding up a palm leaf, was erected in 1947. She commemorates Hungary's liberation from war and fascism. *XI, Szirtes út/Citadella sétány | bus 272, tram 18, 19*

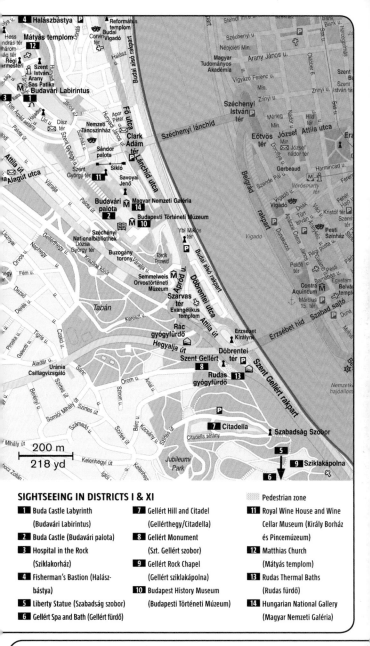

SIGHTSEEING IN DISTRICTS I & XI

1 Buda Castle Labyrinth
(Budavári Labirintus)

2 Buda Castle (Budavári palota)

3 Hospital in the Rock
(Sziklakórház)

4 Fisherman's Bastion (Halász-
bástya)

5 Liberty Statue (Szabadság szobor)

6 Gellért Spa and Bath (Gellért fürdő)

7 Gellért Hill and Citadel
(Gellérthegy/Citadella)

8 Gellért Monument
(Szt. Gellért szobor)

9 Gellért Rock Chapel
(Gellért sziklakápolna)

10 Budapest History Museum
(Budapesti Történeti Múzeum)

░░ Pedestrian zone

11 Royal Wine House and Wine
Cellar Museum (Király Borház
és Pincemúzeum)

12 Matthias Church
(Mátyás templom)

13 Rudas Thermal Baths
(Rudas fürdő)

14 Hungarian National Gallery
(Magyar Nemzeti Galéria)

▣ GELLÉRT BATHS AND SPA (GELLÉRT FÜRDŐ)
(116 C6) (∅ D11–12)

The baths, an Art Nouveau gem, were opened in 1918. The majority of the visitors are tourists who want to experience the magnificent décor. *Mon–Fri 6am–7pm, Sat, Sun until 6pm | XI, Kelenhegyi út 4 (near Hotel Gellért) | www.spasbudapest.com | bus 7, trams 18, 19, 47, 49*

▣ GELLÉRT HILL AND CITADEL (GELLÉRTHEGY/CITADELLA) ⚜
(116 B–C 5–6) (∅ C11)

In addition to Castle Hill, the appearance of Buda is also shaped by Gellért Hill, a 130-m dolomite colossus. In the mid-19th century the Habsburgs built a citadel on the top of the hill. There are wonderful panoramic views of Castle Hill, the city and the Danube from here. *XI, Szirtes út/Citadella sétány | www.citadella.hu | bus 27 or on foot from Gellért tér*

▣ GELLÉRT MONUMENT (SZT. GELLÉRT SZOBOR) (116 B4) (∅ C11)

The statue can be found close to Elisabeth Bridge on Gellért Hill. It commemorates St Gellért (Gerard), who came from Venice in around 1000AD at the request of King Stephen in order to drive forward his programme of Christianisation. Gerard is said to have been nailed to a barrel by a heathen Hungarian and hurled down the hill into the Danube. His statue is enclosed by a semi-circular colonnade. *XI, Gellért hegy | bus 27, trams 18, 19*

▣ INSIDER TIP GELLÉRT ROCK CHAPEL (GELLÉRT SZIKLA-KÁPOLNA) ●

(116 C6) (∅ D11)

The chapel occupies a natural grotto in the side of Gellért Hill. On your way up you can enjoy views of the Danube. Once inside you will find an oasis of tranquility with various niches filled with statues and altars. The church is part of the Paulite monastery that was re-founded in 1989 and is located next door. The four monks enjoy having visitors, and request participation or silence during the services (11am, 5pm and 8pm, Sun also 8.30am). *Daily 9am–8pm | XI, Szent Gellért rakpart (way up near Gellért Baths and Spa)*

RELAX & ENJOY

The ● *Mandala Day Spa*, which also has an Indonesian tea house, offers some top-quality pampering. The services on offer include 20 body massages and more than 30 different facial and body treatments. The *King Lotus Flower package (24,500 Ft.)* consists of an ayurvedic peeling (45 mins) and an ayurvedic massage (75 mins). *Mon–Sun 10am–10pm | III., Ipoly utca 8 | tel. 306 37 00 08 | www.mandaladayspa.hu | underground 2: Léhel tér*

The ticket *Gellért Mix* combines watery fun in Gellért Spa and Bath with a lunch menu or a dinner in the long-established Hotel Gellért. *Lunch menu Tue–Sat noon–3pm, 5990 Ft. | Dinner Tue–Thu 6pm–11pm, 6990 Ft. (in the panorama restaurant) | with food in the pub Mon–Sun noon–3pm and 6pm–11pm | www. gellert.danubiushotels.com | Tickets in the restaurant or at the desk in Gellért Spa and Bath | trams 18, 19, 49*

⑩ HISTORY MUSEUM (BUDAPESTI TÖRTÉNETI MÚZEUM) (119 E5) (*ᗗ C10*)

With the help of archaeological finds this museum traces the city's development from Roman times until the 13th century. The best part is the great Gothic

which Empress Maria Theresa had Buda Castle built. The Royal Wine Museum is an underground encounter: in the vaulted cellars that belonged to the medieval townhouses, Hungary's wines and wine regions are presented over a 1,400 sq m display area, alongside information

A place of tranquillity, high above the Danube: Gellért Rock Chapel

Hall, which was reconstructed from original components. Only a few – albeit culturally and historically important – fragments survive from the Renaissance palace built by King Matthias Corvinus in 1476. *March–Oct daily 10am–6pm, otherwise Tue–Sun 10am–4pm | I, Szent György tér 2 | Buda Castle wing E | www.btm.hu | cable car, bus 16 (castle bus/Várbusz)*

⑪ ROYAL WINE MUSEUM (KIRÁLY BORHÁZ ÉS PINCE-MUZEUM) (119 D4) (*ᗗ B9*)

During the reign of King Matthias Corvinus, Castle Hill was a flourishing little town. After its destruction at the hands of the Turks only ruins remained, on

about medieval viticulture and the former Jewish quarter on Castle Hill, where the wine merchants lived. *May–Sept daily, otherwise Tue–Sun noon–8pm | I, Szent György tér | www.kiralyiborok.com | bus 16 (castle bus/Várbusz)*

⑫ MATTHIAS CHURCH (MÁTYÁS TEMPLOM) (118 C2) (*ᗗ B8*)

The Matthias Church can be found on Szentháromság tér (Trinity Square). This square, at the heart of the Castle Quarter, is the Castle Hill's highest point and its main tourist thoroughfare. The present church, a neo-Gothic gem, was the result of renovations carried out in 1873–96. Inside, visitors can learn about the church's

Oriental flair in Rudas Thermal Bath, one of Budapest's nicest baths

700-year history. It is named after King Matthias Corvinus, who celebrated both of his weddings here with great pomp. During the Turkish occupation it was used as a mosque. The church houses the tomb of King Béla III (reigned 1172–96) and his wife; it is also where, in 1867, the Austrian imperial couple Franz Joseph and Elisabeth (Sisi) were crowned, making them King and Queen of Hungary. A collection of valuable liturgical objects is also on display. *Mon–Fri 9am–5pm, Sat 9am–1pm, Sun 1pm–5pm | I, Szenthárom-ság tér | www.matyas-templom.hu | bus 16 (castle bus/Várbusz)*

13 INSIDER TIP RUDAS THERMAL BATHS (RUDAS FÜRDŐ)
(116 B4–5) (*ɰ C11*)

This Turkish domed building dating from 1556 is situated at the foot of Gellért Hill.

The beautiful baths with a pool dating from 1896 have been comprehensively restored and modernised. The steam room, usually reserved for men, is open to women once a week (Tue 6am–8pm, women only). *Swimming pool Mon–Wed 6am–6pm, Thu–Sun 6am–8pm, Fri, Sat night swimming (10pm–4am) | Steam room men Mon, Wed–Fri 6am–8pm | I, Döbrentei tér 9 | www.budapest gyogyfurdoi.hu | buses 5, 7, 8, 86*

14 HUNGARIAN NATIONAL GALLERY (MAGYAR NEMZETI GALÉRIA) ★
(119 D5) (*ɰ B9*)

Buda Castle is the home of the Hungarian National Gallery, the most important collection of Hungarian art in the country. Among the permanent exhibits are a medieval and a Renaissance lapidarium, Gothic wooden sculptures and panel paintings, late-Gothic winged altars as well as 19th-century paintings and sculptures. Also on display are works by Mihály Munkácsy (1844–1900), the only Hungarian painter to make an international name for himself. He lived and worked in Vienna and Munich and for more than 25 years in Paris. *Tue–Sun 10am–6pm | I, Szent György tér 2 | Buda Castle wings A, B, C and D | www.mng.hu | cable car, bus 16 (castle bus/Várbusz)*

DISTRICTS V & XIII

So much magnificence on just 6.4 sq miles! Almost all of District V (Belváros-Lipótváros) is made up of listed buildings. It is home to some of Hungary's most outstanding attractions.

Wealth, both sacred and profane, is on show in the magnificent buildings near the Parliament Building, including the monumental St Stephen's Basilica. One example of luxurious hotel architecture is the Gresham Palace, housed in a wonderful Art Nouveau building. District V, the heart of Pest, has 27,000 inhabitants,

of which 27 percent are over the age of 65. Such a high percentage of pensioners in a capital's financial and political heart is rare; at the same time many of the residential buildings reflect the difficult social situation of its inhabitants. The flats are mostly owner-occupied, but the various housing associations can't find the money to maintain the properties. To the north is District XIII (Ujlipotváros, population: 108,500), of which Margaret Island is part. This district is the city's green lung. It also has roads with 19th-century townhouses, but it is characterised by working-class tenements and many national minorities, including Serbs, Croats, Poles, Romanians and Armenians.

■ HUNGARIAN ACADEMY OF SCIENCES (MAGYAR TUDOMÁNYOS AKADÉMIA) (119 F3) (*∅ C8–9*)

The Hungarian Academy of Sciences, a striking Neo-Renaissance building from 1862, is one of many institutions founded by reformist politician Count István Széchenyi. It was intended to contribute to strengthening Hungary's national identity. *V, Széchenyi István tér (formerly Roosevelt tér) 9 | tram 2*

KEEP FIT!

A great jogging route around *Margaret Island*. There is no traffic and you have constant views of the Danube's channels. The total distance is around 5km (3 miles) and the track is surfaced throughout. The tram routes 4 and 6 go to the southern end of the island at Margaret Bridge. Those who run from the Buda side (Szabadság tér) from *Gellért Baths* to the citadel (trams 18, 19,

49) will climb a total of 110 m.
A centrally located, modern gym is Astoria Fitness not far from the hotel Astoria. The entrance is easy to miss. It is situated to the left of Casino Senator. *Mon–Fri 6.30am–midnight, Sat/Sun 10am–9pm | weekend ticket 6900 Ft. | V., Károly körút 4 | www.astoriafitness. hu | underground 2: Astoria*

DISTRICTS V & XIII

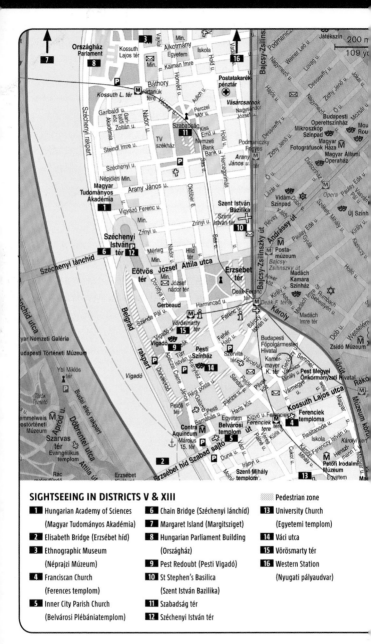

SIGHTSEEING IN DISTRICTS V & XIII

1 Hungarian Academy of Sciences (Magyar Tudományos Akadémia)

2 Elisabeth Bridge (Erzsébet híd)

3 Ethnographic Museum (Néprajzi Múzeum)

4 Franciscan Church (Ferences templom)

5 Inner City Parish Church (Belvárosi Plébániatemplom)

6 Chain Bridge (Széchenyi lánchíd)

7 Margaret Island (Margitsziget)

8 Hungarian Parliament Building (Országház)

9 Pest Redoubt (Pesti Vigadó)

10 St Stephen's Basilica (Szent István Bazilika)

11 Szabadság tér

12 Széchenyi István tér

13 University Church (Egyetemi templom)

14 Váci utca

15 Vörösmarty tér

16 Western Station (Nyugati pályaudvar)

/// Pedestrian zone

2 ELISABETH BRIDGE (ERZSÉBET HÍD) (116 C4) *(ᗯ C–D10)*

The bridge, which was named after Empress Elisabeth of Austria (Sisi) at its opening in 1903, was blown up in 1945. The arch of the bridge, which was rebuilt in 1964, was modelled on the original structure.

3 ETHNOGRAPHIC MUSEUM (NÉPRAJZI MÚZEUM) (119 F1) *(ᗯ C7)*

This magnificent building, stylistically a mix of Renaissance, Baroque and neoclassical influences, was built between 1893–96. The permanent exhibitions are devoted to Hungary's cultural traditions as well as the country's development from primeval society to modern times. *Tue–Sun 10am–6pm | V, Kossuth Lajos tér 12 | www.neprajz.hu | underground 2: Kossuth tér*

4 FRANCISCAN CHURCH (FERENCES TEMPLOM) (117 D3) *(ᗯ D10)*

This Baroque building was constructed in the mid-18th century. The wall paintings and the main altar with its statues are particularly worth seeing. *V, Ferenciek tere 2 | underground 3: Ferenciek tere*

5 INNER CITY PARISH CHURCH (BELVÁROSI PLÉBÁNIATEMPLOM) (117 D3) *(ᗯ D10)*

The Baroque church, built in 1723, has a striking twin-tower façade. It is located in Pest by Elisabeth Bridge and has a late-Gothic choir, a neo-Gothic pulpit and a 15th-century fresco. *Entry during services (daily) | V, Március 15 tér | underground 3: Ferenciek tere*

6 CHAIN BRIDGE (SZÉCHENYI LÁNCHÍD) ● (119 E–F4) *(ᗯ C9)*

The Chain Bridge, lit up to full effect in the evenings, is one of the city's landmarks. The famous suspension bridge was designed by the English engineer William

Tierney Clark, a... vision of Scottis... between 1839–... bridge in the wo... as being the first ...

Elisabeth Bridge lies at the feet of St Gellért

constructed in Budapest. The project was initiated by Count István Széchenyi: apparently, because there was no bridge, it had taken him a whole week to cross the Danube and get to his father's funeral. Crowds of people gather here on St Stephen's Day.

7 MARGARET ISLAND (MARGIT-SZIGET) ★ ● (120 B4–6) *(ᗯ C–D 3–6)*

Budapest's most beautiful park floats like a ship between Margaret Bridge and Árpád Bridge. The island, which is 2.5km (1½ miles) long by less than 500m across, is the city's most popular recreational space.

It owes its name to the daughter of King Béla IV. After the Mongol Invasion he had a convent built, in which his daugh-

A magnificent building for the fatherland: the Hungarian Parliament Building on the Danube

ter Margaret (1242–71) lived for 20 years. The convent's ruins are one of the island's attractions; they can be found near the Water Tower, a Unesco World Heritage Site, which also has a ⚘ viewing platform. The park is reserved for pedestrians and can only be approached by car from the northern tip, where there is a car park. Margaret Island is an ideal spot for joggers, rollerbladers and anyone fancying a walk. During the summer open-air events are held on the outdoor stage. There are many other attractions too, such as the Palatinus Bath, the small zoo, a rose garden and thermal hotels. It is worth lingering at the fountain: the southern one spits water every quarter of an hour, accompanied by classical music. Music can also be heard at the fountain in the northern Japanese garden (every hour on the hour). Carriages and bicycles are for hire. *XIII, trams 4, 6 (Margaret Bridge), buses 26, 34, 106 Árpád Bridge)*

■8 HUNGARIAN PARLIAMENT BUILDING (ORSZÁGHÁZ) ★ ●
(119 F1) (*ᗩ C7–8*)

The dimensions of the Hungarian Parliament Building are enormous: on the side facing the Danube it is 268m long, its dome is 96m (315ft) high, it has 27 gates, 29 staircases and almost 700 rooms. As Hungary's national awareness and self-confidence grew in the 19th century, many Hungarian great minds demanded a suitable 'home for the fatherland'. The location on the Pest-side of the Danube was chosen in order to counterbalance the royal palace, as an expression of the demand for democratic structures. However, it took more than 100 years after construction began for democracy finally to come to the Parliament Building, namely with the elections of 1990. The building works lasted from 1884 until 1902, with the inauguration taking place on the 1000th anniversary of the country in 1896. The architect Imre Steidl (1839–1902) created a bombastic orgy of eclecticism, whose overwhelmingly Gothic Revival style was partly inspired by the Houses of Parliament in London. Once a month, usually on a Friday at 6pm, the chamber orchestra Magyar Virtuózok Kamarazenekar hosts a INSIDER Tip concert in the domed hall *(tickets from ticket offices | Information: bacchus.studio@gmail.com).* The parliament can also be visited as part of a guided tour *(Tours start at the entrance X | Mon–Thu 8am–4.30pm, Fri until 2pm | free for EU citizens).* Its most significant treasure is the much-venerated Holy Crown of Hungary. *V, Kossuth Lajos tér | tel. 1 4 41 49 04 | www.parlament.hu | underground 2: Kossuth Lajos tér, tram 2*

9 PEST REDOUBT (PESTI VIGADÓ)
(116 C2) (ℳ C–D9)

Designed by Frigyes Feszl, the Redoubt was opened in 1865 as a concert hall and ballroom. It has richly ornamented façades and is a neo-romanesque gem. The park in front of the building was cre-

ated by landscape architect Péter Török. *V, Vigadó tér | underground 1: Vörösmarty tér*

10 ST STEPHEN'S BASILICA (SZENT ISTVÁN BAZILIKA) ★ ☆
(123 E5) (ℳ D9)

Construction of this enormous neoclassical church lasted from 1867 to 1906. Its dome is 96m (315 ft) high. It collapsed in 1868 and destroyed the building, which was half-finished at the time. The church's most significant art works are the statue of Alajos Stróbl and the painting 'St Stephen offers Hungary to the Virgin Mary' by Gyula Benczúr. A significant relic, the mummified hand of King Stephen, is exhibited in the basilica. The view from the dome is magnificent.

BOOKS & FILMS

▶ **Fatelessness** – The masterpiece of the winner of the Nobel Prize for Literature, Imre Kertész (1975), this is a semi-autobiographical novel about the experience of a Jewish boy, György Köves, in Ausschwitz. In 2005, it was made into a film by Lajos Koltai under the title *Fateless*.

▶ **In the Land of Blood and Honey** – In 2010 Angelina Jolie made her directorial debut here in Budapest. Run-down streets in district VII were used as the backdrop to this love drama set against the backdrop of the Bosnian War.

▶ **Prague** – With its misleading title, this is a historical novel by American author Arthur Phillips. Set in Budapest, it is about a group of American expatriates at the end of the Cold War.

▶ **Evita** – Scenes for this 1996 movie with Madonna, where Budapest is disguised as Buenos Aires, were filmed in Alkotmány utca (near the Parliament Building).

▶ **The Boy in the Striped Pyjamas** – In this film about the horror of a World War II extermination camp, Budapest is supposed to be Berlin.

▶ **Gloomy Sunday** – In the early 1930s the pianist Resző Seress wrote the song Gloomy Sunday. It plays a central role in the German film of the same name (original title: Ein Lied von Liebe und Tod) with Joachim Król, Ben Becker and Sebastian Koch, set in Nazi occupied Budapest (1999; directed by: Rolf Schübel). By the way, the restaurants in which Seress worked still exist *(Kispipa | V., Akácfa utca 38 and Kulacs | VII., Osvát utca 11).*

You can take a lift up, after which you will also have to climb some stairs. To the right of the entrance is the way down to the treasure chambers. *V, Szent István tér | underground 1: Bajcsy-Zsilinszky út, underground 3: Arany János utca*

ⅠⅠ SZABADSÁG TÉR (123 D4) (*Ⅲ D8*)
Architecture designed to make a splash determines the character of Liberty Square. Somewhat hidden away to the south of the Hungarian Parliament, it is surrounded by some fine buildings, including the striking Art Nouveau American Embassy. This was home to the well-known opponent of the regime, Cardinal Mindszenthy, who lived here in exile right in the heart of the capital from 1956 to 1971. Since being rearranged, the elegant square with its street cafés has become the perfect place for relaxation

LOW BUDGET

▶ EU citizens can visit the *Hungarian Parliament* for free when they present identification.

▶ ● Pensioners (65 and older) can use all public transport for free. Identification has to be shown to conductors.

▶ City tours for under a pound: take the *tram line* 2 (not 2A!) to experience Budapest from its best sides in everyday life (try not to go during rush hour, it gets too full). The best place to sit is on the Danube-side. Line 2 takes around 20 minutes (along Pest's Danube wharves) from the Pest end of Margaret Bridge to the terminus at the Palace of Arts.

and a stroll. A highlight is the interactive sensor-controlled fountain. *V, underground 2: Kossuth Lajos tér, underground 3: Arany János utca*

ⅠⅡ SZÉCHENYI ISTVÁN TÉR
(116 B1) (*Ⅲ C9*)
This square on the Pest side of the Chain Bridge, known as Roosevelt tér until 2011, was designed by the Berlin architect Friedrich Stüler in 1864. It has greatly benefited from the wonderful renovation of the Gresham Palace, one of the city's finest Art Nouveau buildings that belonged to the London-based Gresham insurance company and is now a luxury hotel. The two statues on the pedestals are of the reformist Count István Széchenyi (1791–1860) and the statesman Ferenc Deák (1803–76). *V, tram 2*

ⅠⅢ UNIVERSITY CHURCH (EGYETEMI TEMPLOM) (117 E4) (*Ⅲ D10*)
A Baroque masterpiece close to the market hall in Pest. Construction began in 1725 and was completed in 1771 with the building of the towers. The delicate frescoes and the pulpit are particularly worthy of note. *IV, Egytem tér | underground 3: Ferenciek tere*

ⅠⅣ VÁCI UTCA
(116–117 C–D 2–5) (*Ⅲ D9–10*)
This famous shopping street between Vörösmarty tér, Ferenciek tere and Fővám tér is a magnet for visitors. You will find the usual international chain stores typical of such thoroughfares, as well as a good selection of cafés and bars. The pedestrianised southern section all the way to Fővám tér has its own flair, with an array of interesting shops, including fashion boutiques and antique shops. *V, Vörösmarty tér | underground 1: Vörösmarty tér, underground 3: Ferenciek tere*

15 VÖRÖSMARTY TÉR (116 C2) *(∅ D9)*
In the middle of the square is a memorial to the poet Mihály Vörösmarty (1800–55). The splendid monument is made of high-quality Carrara marble. At the front end, opposite Váci utca, is the renowned Café Gerbeaud. *V, underground 1: Vörösmarty tér*

16 WESTERN STATION (NYUGATI PÁLYAUDVAR) (123 E3) *(∅ D–E7)*
Gustave Eiffel's famous architectural firm created the impressive steel and glass construction of this station, which was completed in 1877. Hungary's first train departed from the old station in 1846. You wouldn't normally expect to find a McDonald's occupying such a splendid work of architecture, but it does here, in a gloriously ornate 1920s-style building adjacent to the station, even claimed by some to be the most beautiful fast-food restaurant on the planet. *V, Teréz körút 57 | underground 3: Nyugati pályaudvar, trams 4, 6*

DISTRICTS VI & XIV

District VI (Terézváros, population: 41,800) boasts a special mix of culture and trendy goings-on. The main highlight here is the boulevard Andrássy út.
High art mingles with popular culture on and around Andrássy út. There are, for example, the Opera House, the Academy of Music, the Kogart Gallery, the Operetta Theatre and the variety club Moulin Rouge. The restaurant and café scene is just as lively, particularly on Liszt Ferenc tér, 'Budapest's Broadway'. With Budapest's most imposing square, Heroes' Square, at the northernmost end of Andrássy út and the adjoining City Park, District XIV (Zugló, population: 61,700)

has two of the capital's attractions to call its own.

1 ANDRÁSSY ÚT ★
(123 E–F 4–5, 124 A–B 2–4)
(∅ D–F 7–9)
The 'Champs Élysées of Budapest' is a manifestation of the new spirit of optimism that grew after 1867. Andrássy út, completed in 1886, consists of three sec-

Perfect starting point for a sightseeing trip: Vörösmarty tér

tions, each of which is a good half-mile long. Up until the Oktogon, the avenue is dominated by residential blocks and shops, with more and more high-fashion labels, from Armani to Zegna, moving into the beautiful, renovated buildings.

From the Oktogon onwards the avenue widens from 34m to 45m. The third section, from Kodály Rotunda to Heroes' Square, is characterised by villas with park-like gardens. *Földalatti* (the 'underground', now underground line 1), which runs under Andrássy út, is the oldest underground railway in mainland Europe, commencing service in 1896. Only London's underground started operating earlier. Both the avenue and the underground are Unesco World Heritage Sites.

railway. Children will also enjoy a ride on the narrow-gauge miniature railway. *April–end of Oct, Tue–Sun 10am–6pm | XIV, Tatai út 95 | www.mavnosztalgia.hu | bus 30*

▪3 HOUSE OF TERROR (TERROR HÁZA) (123 F4) (*𝄡 E8*)

The House of Terror is a memorial to the victims of 20th-century persecution, illustrating the grim decades of Jewish and Roma persecution under the Nazis and further repression and misery under the Com-

The House of Terror is a memorial to the victims of the heinous 20th-century regimes

▪2 'FÜSTI'– HUNGARIAN RAILWAY MUSEUM (MAGYAR VASÚTTÖRTÉ-NETI PARK) (131 D4) (*𝄡 J2*)

The 7-hectare (18-acre) compound behind Western Station is as exciting for children as it is for adults. Among its exhibits are a steam engine built in 1870 (MAV III class 26) and an elegant dining car from the Orient Express dating from 1912. Visitors can power through the landscape in an engine simulator, take a ride in a Tchaika car converted to run on railway lines (for inspections), as well as visit the model

munists. It is housed in the very building where, from 1937 onwards, the grisly Nazi secret police established their headquarters. Countless people were physically and psychologically broken, tortured to death, or executed in the building's basement. After the end of World War II, the Soviet secret service and security organisations took over the premises, torturing, executing or deporting anyone suspected of being an enemy of the state. This chapter of Hungarian history is still very much alive in the minds of many Hungarians. *Tue–Fri*

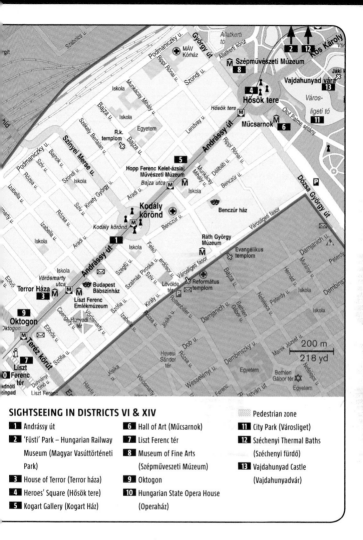

SIGHTSEEING IN DISTRICTS VI & XIV

1 Andrássy út

2 'Füsti' Park – Hungarian Railway Museum (Magyar Vasúttörténeti Park)

3 House of Terror (Terror háza)

4 Heroes' Square (Hősök tere)

5 Kogart Gallery (Kogart Ház)

6 Hall of Art (Műcsarnok)

7 Liszt Ferenc tér

8 Museum of Fine Arts (Szépművészeti Múzeum)

9 Oktogon

10 Hungarian State Opera House (Operaház)

░░░ Pedestrian zone

11 City Park (Városliget)

12 Széchenyi Thermal Baths (Széchenyi fürdő)

13 Vajdahunyad Castle (Vajdahunyadvár)

10am–6pm, Sat, Sun 10am–7.30pm | VI, Andrássy út 60 | www.terrorhaza.hu | underground 1: Oktogon, trams 4, 6

4 HEROES' SQUARE (HŐSÖK TERE) ★
● (124 B2) (ᗯ G6)

Heroes' Square, at the end of Andrássy út, is the city's largest square and combines national pride with aesthetics to produce a successful whole. The 36-m (121ft) column in the middle of the square, the Millennium Memorial, commemorates the 1,000th anniversary of the creation of the Hungarian nation in 896. In 1896, the parliament decided to commission a monument, but 33 years passed before it was finally completed in 1929. Archangel Gabriel stands atop the column. He allegedly ordered King Stephen in a dream to convert Hungary to Christianity; today he watches skateboarders zooming over the square. The statues in the two colonnade arches are of heroes of Hungary's history. The square's other central elements are the Palace of Arts and the Museum of Fine Arts. *VI, underground 1: Hősök tere*

5 INSIDER TIP KOGART GALLERY (KOGART HÁZ) ● (124 B3) (*M F6*)

This beautifully renovated neoclassical villa near the City Park is a feast for the eyes. It houses the art collection of Gábor Kovács, one of Hungary's most successful investment bankers. His passion was for 19th- and 20th-century Hungarian art. As well as seeing fine works of art you can also enjoy eating here: the modern restaurant downstairs is well known for its reasonably priced creative cuisine and excellent service. *Daily 10am–6pm, restaurant noon–2.30pm and 6.30pm–10pm, café 11am–6.30pm | VI, Andrássy út 112 | www.kogart. hu | underground 1: Bajza utca*

6 HALL OF ART (MŰCSARNOK)
(124 B2) (*M G6*)

The large exhibition space in this neoclassical building is illuminated from above by daylight. The Hall of Art does not have any permanent displays, concentrating instead on significant temporary exhibitions. *Tue, Wed, Fri–Sun 10am–6pm, Thu noon–8pm | www.mucsarnok.hu | XIV, Hősök tere | underground 1: Hősök tere, bus 4*

7 INSIDER TIP LISZT FERENC TÉR ●
(123 F4) (*M E8*)

The square's eponym, Franz Liszt, would have enjoyed the café culture all around 'his' square. The monument was erected in 1986, on the 100th anniversary of the composer's death. This attractive corner of town is known as 'Budapest

SPORTY AND STRONG

▶ **Formula 1** – The Hungarian Grand Prix takes place at the Hungaroring at the beginning of August. Almost 80 percent of the track can be seen from the stands. *12 miles northeast of the city centre | www.hungaroring.hu*

▶ **Marathon** – Budapest hosts major running events several times a year. In September and October the city attracts thousands of runners and tens of thousands of spectators and partygoers. The *Nike Budapest Half Marathon* and the *Spar Budapest International Marathon* both start from Heroes' Square. In addition there is the Fun Run for children and the 2-mile Breakfast Run. Margaret Island is the stage for the *Coca Cola Women's Run. www.budapestmarathon. com*

▶ **Football** – The football club nicknamed Fradi (FTC/Ferencváros Torna Club) enjoys cult status. Legendary players of this team (Hungarian champions 28 times) were Flórián Albert and Tibor Nyilasi, to name but two. Museum in the stadium Mon–Fri noon–3pm. *IX., ‹llői út 129 | www.fradi.de.vu | underground 3: Nagyvárad tér*

A monument to the great musician and lots of room for Budapest's trendy side in Liszt Ferenc tér

Broadway'. The trendy cafés and terraces attract visitors until late into the night during the summer months. *VI, underground 1: Oktogon*

8 MUSEUM OF FINE ARTS (SZÉPMŰVESZETI MÚZEUM) ●
(124 B2) (*∅ F–G6*)

The museum, which was completed in 1906, exhibits comprehensive Egyptian, Greek and Roman collections as well as a large selection of Italian paintings from the 13th–18th centuries. The Spanish collection includes no less than 11 works by El Greco. The museum's prints and drawings collection is also of outstanding significance, containing works by Marc Chagall, Lucas Cranach, Albrecht Dürer, Pablo Picasso and Giovanni Battista Tiepolo. Top-quality exhibitions. *Tue–Sun 10am–5.30pm, on every second Thurs until 10pm (with a programme such as jazz) | www.szepmuveszeti.hu | XIV, Hősök tere | underground 1: Hősök tere, bus 4*

9 OKTOGON (123 F4) (*∅ E8*)
Situated at the intersection of Andrássy útca and Térez körút, this octagonal square is among Budapest's most attractive representative squares, lined by 19th-century apartment blocks. *VI, underground 1: Oktogon*

10 OPERA HOUSE (OPERAHÁZ) ●
(123 E5) (*∅ D–E8*)

The magnificent Neo-Renaissance building, constructed between 1875 and 1884, is a work by the architect Miklos Ybl, who also drew up the plans for the entire Andrássy út. It is not just the opera's façade that is stunningly beautiful, but the opulent interior as well. *English-language tours every day at 3pm and 4pm (www.operavisit.hu) | VI, Andrássy út 20 | www.opera.hu | underground 1: Opera, bus 4*

11 CITY PARK (VÁROSLIGET)
(124–125 C–D 2–3) (*∅ G–H 6–7*)

The extensive park is dotted with interesting attractions such as Vajdahunyad, the 'fairytale castle' and the amusement park (Vidám-Park). The zoo and botanical gardens *(Állat-es Növenykert | May–Aug daily 9am–6.30pm, otherwise 6am–4pm | www.zoobudapest.com)* has been extensively modernised. The palm house, aviary and elephant house are particularly attractive, the latter being a domed building constructed with the Zsolnay tiles typical of Hungarian Art Nouveau. One animal that is rarely seen in European zoos is the INSIDER TIP Komodo dragon, which was brought here from Chester Zoo in England in 2008. A hit among teenagers is the ice rink (*Nov–March Mon–Fri 9am–1pm and 4pm–8pm, Sat, Sun 10am–2pm and 4pm–8pm | Olof Palme sétány*). During the summer it is a lake on which you can go canoeing. Gourmets will be attracted to the famous Gundel restaurant, while the Széchenyi Thermal Baths will appeal to wellness fans. *XIV. | www. varosliget.hu | underground 1: Hősök tere and Széchenyi fürdő, Trolleybus 72*

12 SZÉCHENYI THERMAL BATHS (SZÉCHENYI FÜRDŐ) ●
(124 C1–2) (*M G6*)

These baths resemble a magnificent palace complex. There are twelve indoor and outdoor pools. The day clinic offers a broad range of treatments, but the baths are also popular among the fully fit and healthy. It is simply great fun to sit in one of the open-air pools and enjoy the warm thermal water or to get in shape in the fitness suite. You'll need a bit of luck to get a spot by one of the chessboards, however. The spa treatments on offer include Thai massages and foot massages as well as workouts. *Pools daily 6am–10pm, other facilities until 4pm or 7pm | XIV, Állatkerti út 11 | www. budapestgyogyfurdoi.hu | underground 1: Széchenyi fürdő*

13 VAJDAHUNYAD CASTLE (VAJDAHUNYADVÁR) (124 C2) (*M G6*)

This medieval-looking castle in the City Park was built in the 19th century. The architect took his inspiration from Hungary's traditional architectural styles, though it is copied in part from a castle with the same name in Transylvania, Romania. The castle houses a large agricultural museum, but it is visited not just worth its exhibits: the magnificently furnished rooms are also well worth seeing. *Mon–Fri 10am–4pm, Sat, Sun until 5pm | XIV, Városliget | www.mezogazdasagimu zeum.hu | underground 1: Széchenyi fürdő*

DISTRICTS VII & VIII

Vajdahunyad Castle in the City Park

The smart Bar Noir et L'Or is not the only hip venue in Király utca. The trendy street, otherwise known as Budapest's Design Street, is administratively still part of district VI, but it also borders district VII (Erzsébetváros, population: 60,500), the old Jewish Quarter.

As well as providing reminders of the past, District VII is all about optimism

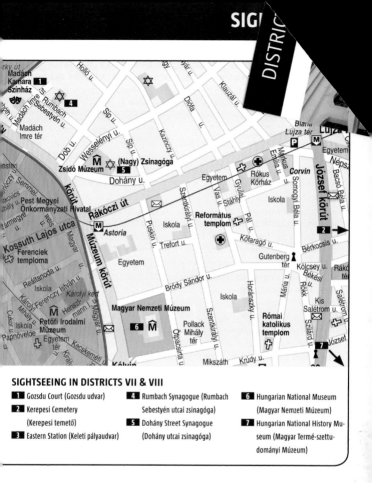

SIGHTSEEING IN DISTRICTS VII & VIII

1 Gozsdu Court (Gozsdu udvar)

2 Kerepesi Cemetery
   (Kerepesi temető)

3 Eastern Station (Keleti pályaudvar)

4 Rumbach Synagogue (Rumbach
   Sebestyén utcai zsinagóga)

5 Dohány Street Synagogue
   (Dohány utcai zsinagóga)

6 Hungarian National Museum
   (Magyar Nemzeti Múzeum)

7 Hungarian National History Museum (Magyar Termé-szettu-
   dományi Múzeum)

for the future. This part of the city used to be dominated by Jewish life and faith, particularly between Király utca and Dohány utca. Today, it is well on its way to combining tradition and modernity. Be they cool designer shops or kosher restaurants, hip bars or shops selling Jewish religious artefacts, magnificently restored houses or still visible decay: the trendy quarter developing here has its own very special flair.

District VIII (Józsefváros, population: 79,500) was home to the country's artist elite in the 1930s and encompasses an extensive working-class neighbourhood. A few years ago it made the headlines as a social flashpoint, but things are now changing. Crime has been reduced significantly through the use of a modern CCTV system. In addition, the measures designed to improve people's living conditions are working. Anyone wanting to see the modernisation process for themselves should explore a few of the streets around Gutenberg tér (near Blaha Lujza tér). Among the rows of houses there are some wonderfully restored buildings. Between them, however, are some that still look just like they did

From 19th-century student accommodation to luxury complex: the magnificent Gozsdu Court

after the war. The district is also associated with the development of Hungarian literature, inextricably linked with the coffee houses of the Royal and New York hotels. The successors of these inspirational venues are the smart Corinthia Grand Hotel Royal and the luxury hotel New York Palace with the restored Café New York.

◗ INSIDER TIP GOZSDU COURT (GOZSDU UDVAR) (117 E1) (ⅅ E9)

Gozsdu Court on the edge of the old Jewish Quarter is an architectural masterpiece, which runs from Király utca 13 to Dob utca. The imposing 19th-century complex consists of seven buildings and six interlinking courtyards. Visitors can stroll from one courtyard to the next. The plan is for the shop spaces to fill up more and more with restaurants, cafés and galleries. In the summer artists and designers liven up the area with the Gouba Bazaar, which is held every Sunday. *VI, Király utca 13 | www.gouba.hu | underground 1, 2, 3: Deák Ferenc tér*

◖ KEREPESI CEMETERY (KEREPESI TEMETŐ) (129 D–E1) (ⅅ H–J 9–10)

Several important 19th-century politicians are buried in this famous cemetery with its parkland setting. Lajos Kossuth, an activist during the Hungarian Revolution of 1848, has an imposing mausoleum. Nearby is a memorial dating from the communist era, where 'worthy fighters' were laid to rest. Poets and thinkers also lie buried here, including the novelist Jókai Mór (1825–1904, lot 18) and the poet Ady Endre (1877–1919, lot 19/1). At the eastern edge of the cemetery, with its tree-lined avenues, is a decaying Jewish cemetery with impressive mausoleums. *During summer daily 7am–8pm, during winter 7.30am–5pm | VIII, Fiumei út 16 | underground 2: Keleti pályaudvar, trams 24, 28*

◗ EASTERN STATION (KELETI PÁLYAUDVAR) (124 C5) (ⅅ G9)

The Eastern Station, built in 1884, with its sculptures and elegant, richly ornamented concourse, is an architectural Neo-Renaissance gem. Well-known artists were involved in the construction of the terminus, which measures 93m in length and 80m in width. The wall paintings feel like they are in a museum wing that has just been reopened after being refurbished.

International trains arrive at the Eastern Station. *VIII, Baross tér | underground 2: Keleti pályaudvar | buses 7, 178*

◼4 RUMBACH SYNAGOGUE (RUMBACH SEBESTYÉN UTCAI ZSINAGÓGA)
(117 E1) (*Ⓜ E9*)

This 'little synagogue', an early work by the Viennese Art Nouveau architect Otto Wagner (1841–1918), has not yet been restored, but it is occasionally open to the public in the summer months. *VII, Rumbach Sebestyén utca 11–13 | underground 1, 2, 3: Deák Ferenc tér*

◼5 DOHÁNY STREET SYNAGOGUE (DOHÁNY UTCAI ZSINAGÓGA) ★
● (117 E2) (*Ⓜ E9*)

This place of worship with its onion domes was built in the mid-19th century in the Byzantine-Moorish style. It is the largest synagogue in Europe and is one of the city's most magnificent buildings. In its courtyard, where the *Holocaust Memorial* by the sculptor Imre Varga is located – a silver, shimmering tree of life – thousands of victims of fascism lie buried. One of the wings houses the *Jewish Museum (Zsidó Múzeum)*, which has a rich collection ranging from Roman times to the 20th century. On the site of the present-day museum stood the house where Theodor Herzl (1860–1904), the founder of Zionism, was born. The synagogue is due to undergo a fair bit of refurbishment. *Mon–Thu 10am–4pm, Fri, Sun 10am–1.30pm | VII, Dohány utca 2 | www.jewinform.hu | underground 2: Astoria, trams 47, 49*

◼6 HUNGARIAN NATIONAL MUSEUM (MAGYAR NEMZETI MÚZEUM) ★
(117 F4) (*Ⓜ E10*)

The striking white building, with a broad flight of steps leading up to the portico with its eight Corinthian columns, was opened as a museum in 1847 after a ten-year construction period. The central exhibition presents Hungary's history from 1000 to 1990. The Hungarians are very aware of their past and nowhere is this better illustrated than in the displays at the National Museum. The regalia of King Stephen, Hungary's first king, were returned in 1978 after spending 30 years in exile in the United States. In 2000 they were moved from the museum to the parliament. The museum's garden is a popular place to come and relax. *Tue–Sun 10am–6pm | VIII, Múzeum körút 14–16 | www.hnm.hu | underground 3: Kálvin tér, trams 47, 49*

Heart of the Jewish quarter: the Dohány Street Synagogue

🟥7 HUNGARIAN NATURAL HISTORY MUSEUM (MAGYAR TERMÉSZET-TUDOMÁNYI MÚZEUM)
(128 C3) (🗺 H12)

The neoclassical museum complex is a fascinating place. The glass floor leading up to the exhibition lets visitors look down on coral reefs, while a 2-ton skeleton of a fin whale hangs under the glass ceiling of the entrance foyer. The main attraction of the mineral and rock collection is an INSIDER TIP opal, which is 15 million years old and weighs 300kg. The sensational discovery was made in the Mátra Mountains in 2006, but it is common, rather than precious, opal, its colouring coming from ferrous materials. The 'Treasures of the Carpathian Basin' collection brings a world of myths and legends to life. *Wed–Mon 10am–6pm | VIII, Ludovika tér 6 | (main entrance on Fogado tér) | www.nhmus.hu | underground 3: Klinikák*

DISTRICT IX

District IX (Ferencváros, population: 59,700) has undergone a revival. Its central attraction is Ráday utca with its cafés, restaurants, boutiques and book and music shops.

The city's young and young at heart like coming here because Ráday utca and the surrounding area have good, affordable living space. At the southern end of this district is a project which, when completed, will confirm the reputation of this part of town as the capital's new cultural centre: the Millennium Quarter with the National Theatre and the Palace of Arts. District IX has its sunny sides, but there is still a lot of work to be done, particularly in the southern residential neighbourhoods. Around 300 houses need demolishing, while 2,500 still have to be renovated.

Liberty Bridge crosses the Danube at Szent Gellért tér

🟥1 LIBERTY BRIDGE (SZABADSÁG HÍD)
(117 D6) (🗺 D11)

This bridge, an impressive iron structure, was built between 1894 and 1896. It was the first crossing over the Danube to reopen after the war in 1946. Since then it has been called Liberty Bridge.

🟥2 INSIDER TIP HOLOCAUST MEMORIAL CENTER (HOLOKAUSZT EMLÉKKÖZPONT) ● *(128 B3) (🗺 F12)*

This complex is worth seeing for its archi-

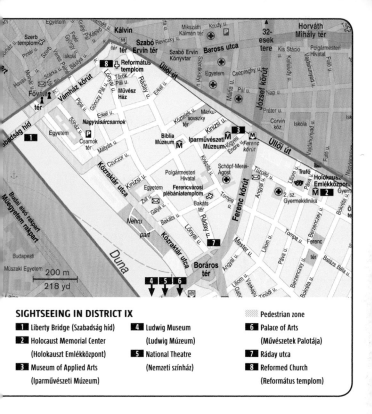

SIGHTSEEING IN DISTRICT IX

1 Liberty Bridge (Szabadság híd)

2 Holocaust Memorial Center (Holokauszt Emlékközpont)

3 Museum of Applied Arts (Iparművészeti Múzeum)

4 Ludwig Museum (Ludwig Múzeum)

5 National Theatre (Nemzeti színház)

6 Palace of Arts (Művészetek Palotája)

7 Ráday utca

8 Reformed Church (Református templom)

Pedestrian zone

tecture alone. It consists of the historic Páva-Synagogue and a new wing dominated by glass. The interior deals with something much darker: the Holocaust in Hungary. In spring 1944, under the rule of Regent Miklós Horthy, 440,000 people were deported to Auschwitz. The Germans and the Arrow Cross Party (the Hungarian Nazis), who came to power in autumn 1944, were responsible for the deaths of tens of thousands more people. In total, the number of murdered Hungarian Jews and Roma is estimated at more than 600,000. Darkness, the light in the cabinets, nightmarish sounds such as the foot steps of concentration camp guards: the exhibition is a journey from darkness to the synagogue's light domed room and out into the light of day. It recalls the warning motto 'principiis obsta', 'nip it in the bud'. *Tue–Sun 10am–6pm | IX, Páva utca 39 | www.hdke.hu | trams 4, 6, underground 3: Ferenc körút*

3 MUSEUM OF APPLIED ARTS (IPARMŰVÉSZETI MÚZEUM)
(128 A3) *(𝄢 F11)*

The museum building, a gem of Hungarian Art Nouveau by Odon Lechner, complete with stunning Zsolnay roof tiling, is outstanding. However, it is also worth seeing the arts and crafts on display, such as the traditional aristocratic costumes and tapestries, Art Nouveau glass and Italian majolica, porcelain, French furniture and silver. *Tue–Sun 10am–6pm | IX, Üllői út 33–37 | www.imm.hu | underground 3: Ferenc körút, trams 4, 6*

because of the national pathos with which it was loaded. The prime minister at the time, Viktor Orbán, crowned the topping-out celebrations and the debates with the sentence: 'The National Theatre has become a national symbol

Colourful tiles, made in Zsolnay, decorate the roof of the Museum of Applied Arts

■4■ LUDWIG MUSEUM (LUDWIG MÚZEUM) (128 A6) (*ω F14*)

Budapest owes its most important collection of contemporary international art to the collectors Irene and Peter Ludwig from Aachen in Germany. Among the artists displayed here are Andy Warhol, Roy Lichtenstein, Robert Rauschenberg and Claes Oldenburg. A second focal point is Hungarian art since 1990. There are also temporary exhibitions. *Tue–Sun 10am–8pm | IX. Komor Marcelli sétány 1 | www.ludwigmuseum.hu | tram 2, commuter train Csepeli HéV*

■5■ NATIONAL THEATRE (NEMZETI SZÍNHÁZ) (128 A6) (*ω F14*)

This building has ruffled some feathers over the years and has split the nation

just like our coat of arms and our national anthem.' The work by architect Mária Siklós is the focus of the new Millennium Quarter. The square in front of the theatre with the park and the open-air bar is a great place to unwind. *Placc. IX, Bajor Gizi Park 1 | www.nemzetiszinhaz.hu | trams 2, 24*

■6■ PALACE OF ARTS (MŰVÉSZETEK PALOTÁJA) (128 A6) (*ω F14*)

The Palace of Arts is the capital's most recent architectural and cultural project of note. The building houses the very modern Béla-Bartók Concert Hall and a festival theatre. In addition it is the home of the Ludwig Museum and the National Dance Theatre. *IX, Komor Marcelli utca 1 | www.mupa.hu | trams 12, 2A*

▪7 RÁDAY UTCA
(117 F5–6) (*ⅢⅢ E11–12*)

The pedestrian zone Ráday utca, which has become a popular destination because of its many cafés and restaurants, begins at Kálvin tér. *underground 3: Kálvin tér*

▪8 REFORMED CHURCH (REFORMÁTUS TEMPLOM) (117 E5) (*ⅢⅢ E11*)

This church, with its impressive glass windows, is a neoclassical work by the famous architect József Hild (1789–1867). He also designed the pulpit and the organ loft. *Daily | IX, Kálvin tér | underground 3: Kálvin tér*

IN OTHER DISTRICTS

AQUAWORLD (131 D3) (*ⅢⅢ 0*)

The dome of this enormous adventure pool is 72m across and five storeys high. The complex also has flumes totalling 900m in length. 15 of the 17 pools are in operation all year round. The surf pool, where bathers can surf on regular boards, is a real hit. *IV, Íves út 16 | (on the Pest side near the new Megyeri Bridge, own exit on the M0) | bus 30 to stop Homoktövis iskola | www.aqua-world.hu*

AQUINCUM (131 D4) (*ⅢⅢ 0*)

Anyone interested in Roman ruins will find some important discoveries in the museum and the outdoor site of Aquincum on the Buda side of the river. You will find, among other things, collections of frescoes and statues, and a mosaic depicting Hercules and Diana. *May–Oct Tue–Sun 10am–5pm, Nov–April until 4pm | III, Szentendrei út 139 | www.aquincum.hu | HÉV: Aquincum, buses 42, 106*

KIRÁLY BATHS (KIRÁLY FÜRDŐ)
(122 C3) (*ⅢⅢ B7*)

The dome of these baths, built in 1565, is the most significant Turkish architectural structure in Budapest. There are no normal swimming pools here, only a thermal bath. Until recently men and women had to bathe separately, but this has been changed now and men and women can use the pool together. The wellness services on offer include massages, a steam room and a sauna. *Daily 7am–7pm | II, Fő utca 84 | www.budapestgyogyfurdoi.hu | bus 86*

MEMENTO PARK (130 C5) (*ⅢⅢ 0*)

For visitors who have no experience of a Communist regime, this sculpture park is a curiosity, while for those shaped by Communism, it marks the end of an era: the ideological figures (Marx, Engels, Lenin) and other monuments of Socialist Realism have found a final resting place in the suburban district of Budatétény. An exhibition commemorates the uprisings against Communism (Budapest, Prague, Warsaw, Berlin). *Daily 10am–sunset | XXII, corner Balatoni út/Szabadkai utca | www.mementopark.hu | bus 150 from Kosztolányi Desző tér (Mon–Fri every 20 mins, Sat, Sun every 30 mins) or from Deák Square in the city centre (near the underground, 11am, July/Aug also 3pm) | Tickets for a programme with a guided tour are available in the bus*

PÁLVÖLGYI CAVE (PÁLVÖLGYI BARLANG) AND SZEMLŐHEGYI CAVE (SZEMLŐHEGYI BARLANG)
(130 C4) (*ⅢⅢ 0*)

Unlike the Buda Castle caves, these caves with their mineral and stalactite formations are a piece of real, fascinating nature. They are 800m (half a mile) apart. It is cold in both caves (11 degrees), so it is a good idea to wear warm clothes and stout footwear. *Pálvölgyi Cave (II, Szépvölgyi út 162 | www.palvolgyi.atw.hu | bus 65 from Kolosy tér to the stop Pálvölgyi cseppkőbarlang)* is the city's longest cave system, measuring 7km (4 miles) in length; 500m of it can be visited as part of a guided tour (no access for children under five). The 300m of *Szemlőhegyi Cave (II, Pusztaszeri út 35 | www.szemlohegyi.atw.hu | bus 29 from Kolosy tér to Pálvölgyi Cave)* are easier to contend with. *Guided tours for both caves run all year round Tue–Thu 10am–4pm on the hour*

OUTSIDE THE CITY

BUDA HILLS (BUDAI-HEGYSÉG)
(130 B–C 4–5) (*0*)
Hikers, mountain-bikers and sightseers will want to leave the city and head straight for the hills. The cog railway *(Fogaskerekűvasút)* dating from 1874 takes around half an hour to get to the top of *Széchenyihegy* (427m/1,401ft). Those of an active disposition can walk up (approx. 45 mins) to *Jánoshegy* (527m/1,729ft), the highest peak of the Buda Hills. It is crowned by the stone ☙ *Elisabeth Tower,* which was erected by Frigyes Schulek, the architect of the Fisherman's Bastion. On clear days visibility can be up to 50 miles! Those who do not feel like walking can take the cog railway to the end and then transfer to the children's railway *(Gyermekvasút),* getting out five stops later. From the seventh station (Hárshegy) there are trails to two further ☙ look-outs.
There is also a chair lift *(Libegő)* that goes up Jánoshegy in 15 minutes. Near the bottom station there is an attractive *campsite (Zugligeti Niche | www.campingniche.hu)* and a place that is meaningful to Germans: in 1989 Imre Kozma, a priest and the former head of the Hungarian Order of Malta, built a camp for people fleeing East Germany near *Thege Miklós út. Cog railway 5am–11pm from the valley station (Szilágyi Erzsébet fasor 47, opposite the Hotel Budapest), can be reached from Széll Kálmán tér (formerly Moszkva tér) by tram line 18 or 56 (two stops) | Bottom station chair lift: Zugligeti út/Csiga út, from Széll Kálmán tér (formerly Moszkva tér) by bus 158*

GÖDÖLLŐ PALACE (KIRÁLYI KASTÉLY)
(131 F3) (*0*)
The Austrian Empress and Hungarian Queen Elisabeth (Sisi) lived in Gödöllő Palace for more than 200 days and nights. She loved this place, which had been made available to her and her husband, Franz Joseph I, in 1867. Its history began when Prince Antal Grassalkovich made the small village of Gödöllő the centre of his estates in the 18th century. The palace's construction began in around 1740. It is the largest Baroque structure in Hungary and, after Versailles, the second-largest Baroque palace in the world. Today Gödöllő (30km/18 miles northeast of Budapest) is a town of 230,000 inhabitants, and the palace and its park are right at the heart of it. The *Palace Museum (daily 10am–6pm | www.kiralyikastely.hu)* has a 170 sq m hall, Sisi's chambers and Hungary's only Baroque theatre. Events and concerts are held in the theatre, the hall and the courtyard. The palace park has been given protected status. There is a photo studio in which you can have your picture taken in period costumes, and a lovely café on the ground floor of the palace. *Information: Tourinform in the palace (tel. 28 419231 | www.gkrte.hu) | commuter*

train/HÉV from Örs vezér tere (terminus of underground 2), in Gödöllő, get out at Szabadság tér

SZENTENDRE (131 D2–3) *(ᗉ 0)*

This lovely town is situated 20km (12 miles) north of Budapest on the Danube famous ceramicist (1902–77). There are some great views from ⚓ *Castle Hill*, which is also the location of Szentendre's oldest church *(Római Katolikus Plébániatemplom)*. Near the Danube promenade you will find the *Promenade Restaurant (Futó utca 4/corner Dunakorzó |*

Hungary's largest Baroque palace: Gödöllő Palace was Empress Sisi's favourite

Bend. Szentendre saw a large number of creative individuals move here at the start of the 20th century. The town's seven orthodox churches were built by Serbian immigrants who had fled from the Turks. The narrow streets and the houses built close together are also characteristic features of Szentendre. On the main square *(Fő tér)* you can see a valuable wrought-iron Memorial Cross of 1752 and *Blagovescenska Church*, constructed in 1752–54. The museum *Károly Ferenczy (Fő tér 6)* exhibits works by local artists. Only a few steps away is the *Margit-Kovács-Museum (Vastagh György utca 1)*, which displays the works by the

tel. 26 312627) in a 17th/18th-century building. Just 3km (2 miles) northwest of Szentendre is Hungary's largest *Ethnographical Museum (Skanzen | Sztra-vodai út | www.sznm.hu | bus from the commuter line terminal station, stop no. 8)* with 80 houses, three churches, seven mills and much more. *Museums in Szentendre spring and summer Tue–Sun 10am–6pm | www.szentendreprogram.hu | Information: Tourinform (Dumtsa Jenő utca 22 | tel. 26 317965 | email: szentendre @tourinform.hu) | commuter line/HÉV (trains every 40 minutes from Batthyány ter) | Boat from Vigadó tér*

FOOD & DRINK

The capital's restaurants leave almost nothing to be desired. Budapest's chefs serve up a good and diverse repertoire in eateries ranging from traditional cafés to modern food temples.

Don't take the word 'café' too literally. Almost all of Budapest's cafés are also restaurants.

Hungarians like to eat their hearts out. Lard and cream are not frowned upon, because the food is meant to taste nice after all, regardless of the calories. Among the popular traditional dishes are breaded meat or fish as well as goulash dishes, which are called *pörkölt*, *paprikás* or *tokány*. Since the country is rich in wildlife, almost every menu will also have game dishes. Hungarians are proud of their culinary traditions and quite resistant towards foreign influences. But change is visibly afoot everywhere, particularly in Budapest. International trends are having an impact and ambitious Hungarian chefs are discovering lighter versions of their local cuisine. They are also focusing more and more on the good meat quality of old Hungarian breeds such as Mangalica pigs and grey cattle. Paprika plays a central role in Hungarian cooking. The spice gives the dishes a characteristic, but mostly moderate heat. By contrast, just a few the fresh chilli peppers served on the side or as part of a salad can be very hot indeed. A pleasing development has taken place with wine. Some typical Hungarian varieties are Kékfrankos, Kékoportó and Kadarka. More and more better wines

From gourmet temples to csárdas with a rustic flair: Budapest's culinary scene is getting more and more interesting

of the Merlot, Pinot Noir and Cabernet Franc varieties are coming on to the market. The wines from the famous wine-growing region of Tokaj-Hegyalja are exquisite, and the dessert wines Tokaj Aszú especially so. Many restaurants and wine bars in Budapest showcase good Hungarian wines. What is particularly nice is that the difference between the shop prices and the restaurant prices is much lower than in the UK, for example. The herbal bitter, Unicum, sold in the striking round bottle, and the fruit brandies (*pálinka*) are served as a digestif after almost every Hungarian meal.

Food and drink festivals have a firm place in Budapest's calendar of events. One such culinary event, held in the City Park in September, is the *Mangalica Festival (www.mangalicafesztival.hu)*. It's all about the meat from this Hungarian pig breed. One strange event is 'Greedy Thursday' celebrated on the day after Ash Wednesday: people go out to restaurants and indulge in gluttony at reduced prices, and that during Lent in Catholic Hungary!

CAFÉS

Anyone wanting to try their way through the Hungarian fruit brandies in Buda Castle in October at the *Pálinka and Sausage Festival (www.palinkaeskolbasz.hu)* needs to be able to hold their liquor. The Wine Festival *(www.winefestival.hu)* is also held in the castle in September; it is accompanied by music and specialities such as cauldron goulash and pogaca.

augusztcukraszda.hu | underground 3: Ferenciek tere

CAFÉ IN HOTEL ASTORIA (117 E3) (*⬚ E10*)
Time has stood still here and guests can experience unadulterated Pest café culture in 'Empire' style. *Daily | Hotel Astoria V, Kossuth Lajos utca 19 | underground 2: Astoria*

Friendly atmosphere and beautiful style: the long-established Centrál Kávéház

CAFÉS

INSIDER TIP AUGUSZT (117 E3) (*⬚ D10*)
Organic milk, butter and eggs butter are used for the delicious cake creations in this long-established café. The excellent quality of the ingredients turns the cakes and ice creams here into exquisite treats that can be enjoyed at the bistro tables. *Closed Sun. | V, Kossuth Lajos utca 14–16 (in the courtyard) | www.*

CENTRÁL KÁVÉHÁZ ★ ●
(117 E4) (*⬚ D10*)
Budapest cheered when this long-established café (near the market hall) was re-opened: in the beautiful, old style, but with a pleasantly casual, airy atmosphere. The service is incredibly friendly. A classic on the menu is a type of pancake known as Gundel palacsinta. *Daily | V, Károlyi Mihály utca 9 | www.centralkavehaz.hu | underground 3: Ferenciek tere*

GERBEAUD (116 C2) (*∅ D9*)
This café on Vörösmarty Square owes its reputation to its magnificent architecture and the brilliant pastry chef Emil Gerbeaud, who opened it in 1884. *Daily | V, Vörösmarty tér 7 | www.gerbeaud.hu | underground 1: Vörösmarty tér*

JEDERMANN (127 F3) (*∅ E11*)
The Goethe Institute is still there, but the old Café Eckermann is now the Jedermann. The new owner is an amateur jazz musician and aims to put on musical events Thu–Sun. There are changing daily dishes for breakfast, lunch and dinner along with the regular menu. *Daily | IX, Ráday utca 58 | underground 3: Ferenc körút, bus 15 (Baross tér), tram 4, 6 (Mester utca)*

NEW YORK KÁVÉHÁZ ★ ●
(124 A5) (*∅ F9*)
The Neo-baroque magnificence of this legendary café is breathtaking. Other cafés are cosier, but to have a coffee in such stylish surroundings or to enjoy a piece of cake or a fruit shake here are experiences not to be missed! *Daily | VII, Erzsébet körút 9–11 | www.newyorkcafe.hu | underground 2: Blaha Lujza tér, buses 7, 178*

RING CAFÉ (123 F4) (*∅ E8*)
Situated on Budapest's most expensive street, this café is smart, yet it has reasonable prices. From breakfasts to cocktails, it's a great place to go. It serves burgers, salads, steaks and good daily specials. *Daily | V, Andrássy út 38 | tel. 1 3315790 | www.ringcafe.hu | underground 1: Oktogon*

SZABADSÁG (123 D4) (*∅ D8*)
The attractive Art Nouveau interior attracts many guests from the surrounding banking and government quarter for breakfast and lunch. The food not only tastes good, it is also a visual treat. *Daily | V, Aulich utca 8 | tel. 13214085 | www.szabadsagkavehaz.hu | underground 2: Kossuth Lajos tér*

RESTAURANTS: EXPENSIVE

One special feature of the capital is its temples of Hungarian cuisine with breathtakingly beautiful décor. They include the *Kárpátia (Daily | V, Ferenciek tere 7–8 | tel. 13173596 | www.karpatia.hu)* (117 D3) (*∅ D10*) and the *Matthias Cellar (Mátyás Pince | Daily | V, Március tér*

15, at the Pest end of Elisabeth Bridge | tel. 1 2 66 80 08) (117 D4) (*∅ D10*) with its outstanding gypsy band. These addresses are a visual treat, but be aware that they are also the preferred destinations of travel groups and tourists.

CAFÉ PIERROT (118 C2) (*∅ A8*)

With its vaulted ceilings, this restaurant on Castle Hill combines historical charm with an elegant bistro ambience. Accompanied by piano music, it serves modern Hungarian cuisine, such as a 'goose liver trilogy', Hortobágy palacsinta and a 'game duet with Waldorf salad'. *Daily | I, Fortuna utca 14 | tel. 1 3 75 69 71 | www. pierrot.hu | bus 16 (Castle bus/Várbusz)*

CSALOGÁNY 26 ★ (122 B4) (*∅ B7*)

Everything here is right: the Franco-Hungarian cuisine, the service and the relaxed atmosphere. You can enjoy the delicious dinners, but also a lunch menu for around ten euros. *Closed Sun, Mon | I, Csalogány utca 26 | tel. 1 2 0178 92 | www.csalogany26.hu | underground 2: Batthyány tér*

KÉPIRÓ (117 E4) (*∅ E10*)

The Képiró doesn't just look to Paris when it comes to ambience. The cuisine combines French, Hungarian and other influences to come up with its own blend. *Daily | V, Képiró utca 3 | tel. 1 2 66 04 30 | underground 3: Kálvin tér*

NOIR ET L'OR (123 E5) (*∅ E9*)

A French chef and an elegant setting in black and gold make for a great venue for an extended breakfast or an evening with good food and wine. Apart from dishes with a Mediterranean touch this restaurant also serves Hungarian fare such as veal paprikash. The dessert *Noir et l'Or*

GOURMET RESTAURANTS

Bock Bisztro ★ (123 F5) (*∅ E8*)

József Bock from Villány, one of the country's best winegrowers, occupies a top spot in Budapest's gastronomy with his Bock Bisztro. The food delivers interesting accents, but at its core is traditional Hungarian fare. Entrees starting at 12 euros. *Closed Sun | VII., Erzsébet körút 43–49 | tel. 1 3 21 03 40 | www.bockbisztro.hu | underground 1: Oktogon, trams 4, 6*

Costes ★ (127 F2) (*∅ E11*)

The first restaurant in Budapest to be awarded a Michelin star, located on the popular Ráday utca. It has an elegant art deco ambience and exquisite cuisine with exotic accents. The eight-course dégustation menus at fair prices are particularly highly recommended. Entrees starting at 18 euros. *Closed Mon, Tue | IX., Ráday utca 4 | tel. 1 2 19 06 96 | www. costes.hu | underground 3: Kálvin tér*

Onyx (123 D6) (*∅ D9*)

Guests are treated to an opulent dining ambience with exquisite food. One of the delicious options is: goose liver torte with apple sauce and walnut pastry. The restaurant provides a modern take on Hungarian cuisine and has one Michelin star. Entrees starting at 24 euros. *Closed Sun | V., Vörösmarty tér 7–8 | tel. 1 4 29 90 23 | www.onyxrestaurant. hu | underground 1: Vörösmarty tér*

Diners eat with a view of the Danube and Castle Hill in the boat restaurant Spoon

selection is delicious. *Daily | VII, Király utca 17 | tel. 1 4 13 02 35 | www.noiretlor.hu | underground 1, 2: Deák Ferenc tér*

SPOON ★ ●

(116 B–C2) *(C9–10)*

The elegant floating restaurant and café is anchored opposite the Hotel Intercontinental. The great view of Buda Castle and the good Hungarian-international cuisine make a visit to this restaurant a particular pleasure. *Closed Sun | V, Vigadó tér | tel. 1 4 11 09 33 | www.spooncafe.hu | tram 2*

RESTAURANTS: MODERATE

BAGOLYVÁR (124 B2) *(G6)*

Hungarian home-cooked fare of a high standard, always freshly prepared. The restaurant is part of the Gundel gastronomic family. *Daily | XIV, Állatkerti út 2 | tel. 1 4 68 31 10 | www.bagolyvar.com | underground 1: Hősök tere*

INSIDER TIP **BALETTCIPŐ**

(123 E4–5) *(D8)*

A mix between a bar, a restaurant and a café. Here, close to the opera house, you will find an international audience in a smart, casual ambience. The DJs play their music on Fridays and Saturdays. The restaurant's speciality is burgers and they are the best in the whole city. *Daily | VI, Hajós utca 14 | tel. 1 2 69 31 14 | www.balettcipo.hu | underground 1: Opera*

CAFÉ KÖR (123 D5) *(D9)*

Almost like in Paris: a café-restaurant with a bistro atmosphere. It tends to get very full in the evenings, so it's a good idea to book a table in advance. *Closed Sun | V, Sas utca 17 | tel. 1 3 11 00 53 | www.cafekor.com | underground 3: Arany János utca*

INSIDER TIP **FLAMENCO** (123 F5) *(E9)*

Folklore shows are designed to make this oasis with its attractive courtyard a

LOCAL SPECIALITIES

▶ **Barackos gombóc** – dumplings made of potato dough, stuffed with an apricot

▶ **Dobos-torta** – famous cake made of six sponge layers, chocolate butter cream and a caramel glaze

▶ **Gesztenyepüré** – chestnut dessert

▶ **Gulyásleves** – goulash soup (photo right)

▶ **Gundel-palacsinta** – palacsinta (pancake) with filling (walnuts, candied orange peel, raisins and rum) and a chocolate sauce

▶ **Halászlé** – fish soup, typically consisting of several types of fish, such as carp, catfish and cod

▶ **Hortobágyi palacsinta** – palacsinta with a filling made chicken breast mince, sour cream, onions, paprika and tomatoes

▶ **Langós** – deep-fried flat bread made with a yeast-potato dough, served with a variety of fillings

▶ **Letcsó** – vegetable dish made of tomatoes, peppers and onions, served as a side or a stew

▶ **Paprikás csirke** – chicken, fried with onions, garlic and paprika powder and served with a sour cream sauce (photo left)

▶ **Rántott** – breaded dishes (meat or fish). There are also battered vegetables, mostly served as a starter, such as *rántott karfiol* (cauliflower) or *rántott gombafejek* (mushrooms)

▶ **Töltött káposzta** – Hungarian stuffed cabbage. Further typical *töltött*-dishes are: stuffed onions *(töltött hagyma)* and peppers *(töltött paprika)*

▶ **Túrós rétes** – curd cheese strudel, served in many sweet and savoury variations

▶ **Vörösboros megyleves** – popular fruit soup, the 'tipsy morello cherry soup'

---

venue with a very Hungarian feel. The dishes of this garden restaurant are typically Hungarian as well as Italian and Israeli. The menu lists kebabs as well as carpaccio and hummus and pizza from a stone oven, served outdoors. *Daily | VII, Dob utca 55/Ecke Kertész utca 35 |* *tel. 1 41 3 05 67 | underground 1: Oktogon, tram 4, 6*

INSIDER TIP ▶ MERLIN *(117 D–E2) (∅ D9)*
The productions in this theatre-cum-club are cosmopolitan, and the same goes for its restaurant, which has a colourful

choice of dishes, from tapas to Malaysian vegetable rice and chicken with tarragon. The selection for vegetarians is also considerable. Fri and Sat are particularly busy – and stay busy until late at night. *Daily | V, Gerlóczy utca 4 | www.merlin szinhaz.hu | underground 2: Astoria or Deák Ferenc tér*

OSTERIA FAUSTO'S
(123 E6) (*ØØ E9–10*)
This smart restaurant can be relied upon for serving good Mediterranean cuisine. Classics include the Italian fish soup and the home-made ravioli. *Closed Sat afternoons and Sun | VII, Dohány utca 5 | tel. 1 2 69 68 06 | www.osteria.hu | underground 2: Astoria*

PESTI LÁMPÁS (117 E4) (*ØØ D10*)
You can sit in the stylish courtyard during the summer months. The service is friendly and the prices are very reasonable. Upscale Hungarian-international dishes include pike-perch with porcino ragout, mangalica chops with potato fritters and wild duck with polenta and fig mostarda. Live music on Fridays. *Closed Sun | V, Károlyi Mihály utca 12 | tel. 1 2 66 95 66 | www.pestilampas.hu | underground 3: Ferenciek tere*

RIVALDA ★ (122 B5–6) (*ØØ B9*)
The drapes and the pretty blue, ochre and orange tones combine well with the good cuisine to produce a successful whole at this restaurant on Castle Hill. The atmosphere is smart, but not formal; it's a fun place to eat and in the evenings there's relaxing musical accompaniment. During the summer they also have a nice café in the former monastery courtyard. *Daily | I, Színház utca 5–9 | tel. 1 4 89 02 36 | www.rivalda.net | bus 16 (Castle bus/Várbusz)*

Smart, but relaxed: the Rivalda on Castle Hill

ROBINSON (124 B2) (*ØØ G6*)
An idyll on the lake: in the City Park under trees, not far from the colonnades on Heroes' Square. Perfect for eating outside on the terraces, but those who wish to can dine indoors in an elegant setting (4pm–6pm café only). *Daily | XIV, Város-ligeti tó | tel. 1 4 22 02 22 | www.robinsonrestaurant.hu | underground 1: Hősök tere*

SOUL CAFÉ (117 F5) (*ØØ E11*)
The trendy neighbourhood of Ráday utca is home to this smart café with a strong Mediterranean ambience. The chef is inspired by international cuisine, and accompanying the good food are the wines from the best Hungarian vintners; excellent cocktails too. During the summer there's outdoor seating terrace in the pedestrian zone. *Daily | IX, Ráday utca 11–13 | www.soulcafe.hu | underground 3: Kálvin tér*

VÖRÖS POSTAKOCSI (117 F5) (*ØØ E11*)
Those who wish to experience Hungarian cuisine along with a Hungarian atmosphere, should try the 'Red Stagecoach'. You can sample meat from mangalica pigs and grey cattle, and there's music and folklore in the evenings. Beer and

meat lovers will want to go to the *Beer Cellar*. Alongside a large choice of beers, they have steaks from Argentinean Angus cattle. Again, you can eat outside during the summer. *Daily | IX, Ráday utca 15 | tel. 1 2 17 67 56 | www.vorospk.com | underground 3: Kálvin tér, bus 15*

RESTAURANTS: BUDGET

A LA GALETTA CREPERIE (123 E3) *(ɯ E7)*
Crèpes and galettes: these specialities are the passion of the French proprietor Christophe. Whether it is savoury or sweet, as a main dish, dessert or snack: this place serves these fine creations, deliciously prepared. A glass of cider is a must of course. *Closed Mon | VI, Szondi utca 11 | tel. 1 3 02 69 25 | bus 73, trams 4, 6*

AMSTEL RIVER CAFÉ (117 D3) *(ɯ D10)*
Small and cosy, near Váci utca, Dutch pub atmosphere. The cuisine is good, the daily specials can be found on a blackboard. *Daily | V, Párizsi utca 6 | tel. 1 2 66 43 34 | www.amstelrivercafe.com | underground 3: Ferenciek tere*

INSIDERTIP **LE BAR** ☺ (117 E3) *(ɯ E10)*
Vegetarians and those with a penchant for organic food won't find much to satisfy their needs in Budapest. *Le Bar* is the exception. The selection is large, but the décor is wanting. The fact that the food is served on disposable plastic tableware doesn't exactly suit the eco image, but the prices are low and the dishes change on a daily basis. *Closed Sat/Sun | V, Múzeum körút 19 | underground 2: Astoria*

HUMMUS BAR (121 F5) *(ɯ E8)*
The top floor is a cosy place to sit, but if you're in a hurry you can eat at the bar. This place serves fresh, delicious hummus along with free flat bread, olives and onions. *Daily | VII, Kertész utca 39 | tel. 1 2 53 44 74 | www.hummusbar.hu | underground 1: Oktogon, trams 4, 6*

INSIDERTIP **JUBILEE** (123 D3) *(ɯ D7)*
This casual café-restaurant has a Mediterranean flair. A good breakfast selection, lots of snacks (baguettes, ciabatta), salads, home-made soups and Nanna's home-made ravioli. *Daily | V, Szent István körút 13 | tel. 1 7 89 33 57 | www.cafejubilee.hu | trams 2, 2A: Jászai Mari tér, underground 3: Nyugati Pályaudvar*

KARMA (121 F4) *(ɯ E8)*
The menu of this café restaurant has creations inspired by Mediterranean

LOW BUDGET

▶ In the ● *Great Market Hall* (1st floor) you can buy savoury or sweet *langós* for 2 euros (flat bread made from a yeast-potato dough with, for example, sour cream and cheese) – delicious! *IX., Vámház körút 1–3 | trams 2, 47, 49 |* **(127 E2)** *(ɯ D–E11)*

▶ Only a stone's throw from Liszt Ferenc tér is *Kiadó*. Nice pub atmosphere, breakfast, dishes between 3 and 6 euros. *Daily from 9am | VI., Jókai tér 3 | tel. 1 3 31 19 55 | underground 1: Oktogon |* **(123 F4)** *(ɯ E8)*

▶ There are many vegetarian dishes to choose from in *Főzelekfaló* (2–4 euros). Meat dishes, soups, salads and sweet treats too. *Closed Sun | VI., Nagymező utca 18 | no tel. | underground 1: Opera |* **(123 E4)** *(ɯ E8)*

and Asian cuisine, such as chicken kebabs with avocado-cucumber relish. In addition there's live music and cocktails. *Daily | VI, Liszt Ferenc tér 11 | www.karma budapest.com | tel. 1 413 67 64 | underground 1: Oktogon*

MENZA (121 F4) (*M E8*)

Merges downtown sophistication with the relaxed atmosphere of a 1960s coffee bar. The diverse menu lists many soups and salads, main dishes ranging from penne to *lángos*, duck and goose liver. The palacsinta with quark covered in vanilla sauce and meringue is delicious. Inexpensive daily specials. *Daily | VI, Liszt Ferenc tér 2 | tel. 1 413 14 82 | www.men zaetterem.hu | underground 1: Oktogon*

OKAY ITALIA (121 E3) (*M D7*)

Those wishing to eat Italian food at moderate prices (pizza, pasta, classics like saltimbocca), are in the right place in the two restaurants near the Western Station. *Daily | V, Nyugati tér 6 | tel. 1 332 69 60; Szent István körút 20 | tel. 1 349 29 91 | www.okayitalia.hu | underground 3: Nyugati pályaudvar*

VAPIANO (114 C2) (*M D9*)

Budapest also has an upscale Italian snack bar. It's quick, freshly prepared and tastes good: based on this motto, guests are given a chip card and then the pasta, pizza or salad follows. *Daily | V, Bécsi utca 5 | www.vapiano.hu | underground 1: Vörösmarty tér, U-Bahn 2: Deák Ferenc tér*

VEGETARIUM G (115 D4) (*M D10*)

The tasty selection and the ambience also attract those who are not vegetarians or vegans. A large selection, the cuisine is internationally inspired. Alcoholic beverages such as wine and fruit brandies are also served. *Daily | V, Cukor utca 3 | tel. 1 484 08 48 | www.vegetarium.hu | underground 3: Ferenciek tere*

Cocktail al fresco: Café restaurant Karma on Liszt Ferenc tér

SHOPPING

CITY **WHERE TO START?**

Váci utca and its side streets are a shopping Mecca. International fashion and shoe labels are represented here, as are small Hungarian shops. Turn left or right in the northern section and you will be able to extend your shopping spree for many more discoveries. Vörösmarty tér is home to the shopping centre Váci 1, if you turn right you will find yourself in the small Deák Ferenc utca ('Fashion Street'). If you want to find out what Budapest has to offer in terms of international luxury brands, explore the boulevard **Andrássy út**. The largest shopping centre is the **Westend City Center** at the Western Station.

The Váci utca pedestrian zone in Pest is Budapest's best-known shopping street, but the elegant boulevard Andrássy út with its cafés and restaurants and the magnificent architecture is undoubtedly the city's most attractive shop-window. Váci utca is packed with shops selling everything from fashion and beauty brands to porcelain, folklore and souvenirs. The southern section (Szabad sajtó út to Fővám tér) is quieter and you will find smaller shops with Hungarian products. Király utca, which runs parallel to Andrássy út, is on the way to becoming a top address for design fans with its furniture and home furnishings shops. The 4.5-km (3-mile) Grand Boulevard (Nagykörút) between Margaret Bridge and Petőfi Bridge is still a little piece of

Whether it's culinary treats, glass and porcelain or fashion and young designs: you can get almost anything in Budapest

old Budapest with nostalgic shops, which are, however, gradually disappearing. The young in particular are drawn to shopping centres with their ranges of fashion outlets, restaurants and cinemas. Shops are usually open Mon–Fri 10am–6pm, Sat until 1pm or 2pm. Food shops open earlier. Shopping centres close at 8pm and are also open at weekends.

Among the best souvenirs are delicious culinary items such as winter salami *(téliszalámi)*, the famous goose liver *(libamáj)*, Szamos marzipan, Hungarian wines, fruit brandies *(pálinka)* – especially the apricot brandy *(barackpálinka)* – and the herbal liqueur Unicum. Other good souvenir or gift items are handicrafts (pottery, embroidery, lace, blankets) and tableware (porcelain, ceramics). High-quality porcelain comes from Herend, which specialises in hand-painted and gilded items pieces is the Hungarian equivalent of Germany's Meissen. The products made by Zsolnay are a less expensive alternative. Another good choice is Hungarian glass, such as

Shopping cult with a cinema and a roof terrace: the Westend City Center in Pest

crystal glasses. The antique shops and galleries are also of interest. Reputable dealers can be found in Falk Miksa utca and in Váci utca.

ANTIQUES & GALLERIES

In the realm of art and antiques, Budapest is no longer a place where bargains are easy to come by, but for non-experts the shops are nonetheless a pleasure and you will definitely be able to find something you like during your shopping outings.

BÁV

Something of old Budapest is provided by the various branches of BÁV (Bizományi Kereskedőház). You will find all kinds of antiques, trinkets and treasures, largely from the 18th and 19th centuries, including Art Nouveau and Art deco items. *II, Frankel Leó utca 13* (gold, silver, porcelain) *| trams 4, 6* (122 B2) *(ψ B6)*; *V, Váci utca 74* (carpets, art, jewellery) *| underground 3: Ferenciek tere* (117 D4) *(ψ D10)*

DUNAPARTI AUKCIÓSHÁZ ÉS GALÉRIA (117 D3) *(ψ D10)*

The whole spectrum of art objects. *V, Váci utca 36 | www.dunapartiaukcioshaz.hu | underground 3: Ferenciek tere*

INSIDER TIP KOLLER GALÉRIA (122 B4) *(ψ B8)*

The doors of Budapest's first private gallery opened in 1980. Its founder, György Koller, has created a really special place, with art is displayed over three beautifully appointed floors and there is also a pleasant sculpture garden. The gallery exhibits classic works, but also works by young artists. *I, Mi-*

hály Táncsisc utca 5 | www.kollergaleria. hu | bus 16 (castle bus/Várbusz)

PINTER ANTIKVITÄT (123 D3) *(ffff C7)*
This antique shop looks small from the street, but it has ample space in which it sells paintings, furniture, candleholders and the like. *V, Falk Miksa utca 10 | www. pinterantik.hu | trams 2, 4, 6*

BOOKS & MUSIC

INSIDER TIP ALEXANDRA KÖNYV ÉS BOR (123 E5) *(ffff E8)*
A very special kind of bookshop: you can sit in cosy sofas in the café corner of this elegant shop. Apart from books (including English ones) and CDs, you can purchase Hungarian wines here. *VI, Andrássy út 35 | underground 1: Opera*

SHOPPING & LEISURE CENTRES

ASIA CENTER (131 D–E4) *(ffff 0)*
Covering more than 200,000 sq m this is an enormous Far Eastern emporium. There are more than 500 retailers, selling mostly inexpensive items. Those who like browsing around should be able to pick up some bargains here. *XV, Szentmihályi út 167–169 | www.asiacenter.hu | buses 173 and 173E to Nyírpalota út, from there it is 150m on foot*

MOM PARK (126 A2) *(ffff A10)*
Large shopping centres are particularly popular with teenagers. MOM Park is a multi-functional centre with many entertainment facilities. *XII, corner Alkotás út/ Csörsz utca | www.mompark.hu | tram 61*

INSIDER TIP VÁCI 1 (116 C2) *(ffff D9)*
This Art Nouveau gem is the dominant building on the right-hand side of Vörösmarty tér when coming from

Váci utca. During the communist era it housed the Luxus department store, which fell into oblivion after the fall of Communism. The new, smart shopping complex, which also features a panorama terrace, has space for 70 clothes shops and Hungary's first Hard Rock Café. *V, Váci utca/corner Vörösmarty tér | underground 1: Vörösmarty tér*

WESTEND CITY CENTER ★
(123 E2–3) *(ffff D–E 6–7)*
This 200 million-euro project has developed into a lively centre at the heart of Pest, next to the Western Railway Station. This bright temple of consumerism has hundreds of shops, a hotel, a cinema and several snack bars and restaurants. Clothing shops are the most prevalent, but there are also some specialist retailers such as a good spice shop and shops selling Hungarian specialities. With a roof terrace. *VI, Váci út 1–3 | (near West-*

★ **Westend City Center**
Budapest's largest shopping centre → p. 69

★ **Folkart Centrum**
Hungarian folk art on two floors → p. 70

★ **Great Market Hall**
Paprika and salami under steel and glass → p. 70

★ **Tamás Náray**
The shop of this haute couture designer is as attractive as his creations → p. 71

★ **Herend Porcelain**
Hungary's finest porcelain → p. 73

MARCO POLO HIGHLIGHTS

ern Station) | www.westend.hu | underground 3: Nyugati pályaudvar

FOLKLORE

FOLKART CENTRUM ★
(117 D4) (*⊞ D10–11*)
The entire spectrum of Hungarian handicrafts. On sale here you will find hand-woven blankets, dolls, colourfully painted crockery and lots of ceramics. *V, Váci utca 58 | www.folkartcentrum.hu | underground 3: Ferenciek tere*

MARKETS & DELICATESSEN

INSIDER TIP **CULINARIS** (124 A4) (*⊞ E8*)
Hunyadi tér is a culinary oasis with a market hall, street vendors and the Culinaris delicatessen. In just a small space this shop sells delicacies from all over the world. If you wanted a picnic, for example, you could get your ingredients here: from hams and caviar to cheese and wine. Only opens at noon on Mon *I, Hunyadi tér 3 | www.culinaris.hu | underground 1: Vörösmarty utca*

MARKET HALL BATTHYÀNY TÉR
(118 D1) (*⊞ B8*)
One of the city's attractive old market halls. ☙ Some of the seats in the café afford great views of the Parliament Building on the other side of the Danube. Popular with students: the palacsinta shop *Nagymama*, which is open around the clock. *I, Batthyàny tér 5 | underground 2: Batthyány tér*

GREAT MARKET HALL (KÖZPONTI VÁSÁRCSARNOK) ★ ●
(127 E2) (*⊞ D–E11*)
You will get the best view of the 150-m long market hall with its two aisles from one of the transverse corridors on the top floor. Designed by Samu Pecz, this beautiful building was extremely modern at the time it was built in the 1890s. Even though

The Great Market Hall is a great place to go shopping and also an architectural highlight almost no visitor to Budapest leaves without seeing it, it is not an establishment for tourists, but one of the country's most important markets with a huge variety of stalls. Whether it's fruit, vegetables, meat or fish: this place sells everything the heart desires. If you're looking for souvenirs, you can buy them on the first floor. Haggle! *IX, Vámház körút 1–3 | trams 2, 47, 49*

FASHION & DESIGN

INSIDER TIP **ARIOSO** (117 E1) *(ﾉﾉ D9)*

An absolute dream of an interiors shop, that also sells plants and cut flowers. The Swiss owners have created an unusual aesthetic oasis that combines nature and design (largely Lambert) in a wonderful way. The special charm of the place is rounded off by the café *La Petite Française (www.lapetitefrancaise.com),* where you can enjoy delicious sweets or a small snack – in the cosy courtyard when the weather is good. *VII, Király utca 9 | www.arioso.hu | underground 1, 2: Deák Ferenc tér*

DEÁK FERENC UTCA
(116–117 C–D2) *(ﾉﾉ D9)*

This road is also known as 'Fashion Street', because a large number of clothing brands have opened shops here, such as Hugo Boss, Prada, Tommy Hilfiger and Dolce & Gabbana. *V, Deák Ferenc utca | underground 1, 2: Deák Ferenc tér*

INSIDER TIP **EVENTUELL GALLERY**
(117 D4) *(ﾉﾉ D10)*

It's definitely worth calling in here, particularly of you like colourful creations. The fabrics and rugs, curtains and cushions, bags, jewellery and various accessories and furniture items are designed exclusively for this shop by its own team of designers. Every item in the collection is a hand-made limited-edition piece. *V, Nyáry Pál utca 7 | www.eventuell.hu | trams 2, 2A*

FREGOLI ☺ (117 E5) *(ﾉﾉ E11)*

The young, environmentally friendly designer Ipek Türkoglu sells highly original bags, purses and belts in her small shop. Everything is made from the rubber of bicycle inner tubes, and it's amazing what smart things she manages to fashion from this material. They are sold under the label Balkantango. *V, Bástya utca 8–10 | www.fregolishop.com | underground 3: Kálvin tér*

GLAMOUR (123 E4) *(ﾉﾉ E8)*

A fascinating shop selling unusual items: wigs and fashion, fancy dress, feather boas and fetching underwear. Many stars from the nearby theatre shop here, because the owner will tailor anything to fit. *VI, Nagymező utca 6 | underground 1: Opera*

INSIDER TIP **INSITU** (117 E3) *(ﾉﾉ E10)*

An incredible shop! Clothes and accessories of Hungarian brands such as Balkantango, top-class electronic gadgets such as fish-eye cameras, fun jewellery made of plastic insects, colourful wristwatches and, upstairs, a storeroom where it's okay to rummage around. *V, Múzeum körút 7 (in the passage) | www.insitu.hu | underground 2: Astoria*

MONO FASHION (117 E3) *(ﾉﾉ E10)*

A trendy shop with designer fashion and accessories at affordable prices. Labels such as Nubu, Artista and further young designers are represented here. *V, Kossuth Lajos utca 20 | monofashion.hu | underground 2: Astoria*

TAMÁS NÁRAY ★
(117 D–E 3–4) *(ﾉﾉ D10)*

His fashion shows take place in fancy locations such as Ybl Palace: the haute couture designer Tamás Náray inhabits a world of fabrics and colours. His shop is a visual feast and his designs thrill women and men alike. *V, Károlyi Mihály utca 12 | www.naraycompany.hu | underground 3: Ferenciek tere*

 ☺
(123 E6) (*E9*)

A creative centre for environmentally-conscious design, exhibitions, art and textile prints. You can buy clothes such as T-shirts, as well as bags, lampshades and jewellery from 17 different designers. The coffee available in the café comes from a fair trade project. *VII, Rumbach Sebes-tyén utca 10 | www.printa.hu | underground 1, 2, 3: Deák Ferenc tér*

INSIDERTIP RETROCK DE LUXE
(117 E4) (*E10*)

Anyone turning into Ferenczy I. utca from the ring road Múzeum körút near the Astoria hotel will find themselves in a rather dark little street. The ray of hope here is the sign saying 'Retrock', a hip clothing store well known among the youth of Bu-

dapest. At the end of the street turn left into Henszlmann Imre utca (along the park). That's where you will find Retrock de Luxe, which also carries creations by young Hungarian designers. The shops are an interesting little world of their own. *V, Henszlmann Imre utca 1 | www.retrock.com | underground 2: Astoria*

V-DESIGN ART STUDIO
(117 D4) (*D10*)

Valéria Fazekas's hat creations are worn all over the world. In her small studio she creates everyday headwear as well as more eccentric items for those special occasions. *V, Váci utca 50 | www.valeriafazekas.com | underground 3: Ferenciek tere*

WAMP DESIGN MARKET
(116 D1) (*D9*)

It is predominantly young designers and artisans who sell their goods at the *Wasárnapi Művést Piac market,* or Wamp for short. Usually on the 3rd Sunday of the month (10am–6pm), Nov–March, under Erzsébet tér in *Gödör Club,* a popular cultural centre with music events, exhibitions and a café. *Erzsébet tér | underground 1, 2: Deák Ferenc tér | www.wamp.hu*

KATTI ZOÓB **(123 D3)** (*D7*)

The former costume-designer Katti Zoób is the female figurehead of Hungarian haute couture and her shop the shining beacon on the Grand Boulevard. The prices for her creations are quite high, but browsing is free. *V, Szent Istvan körút 17 | www.kattizoob.hu | underground 3: Nyugati Pályaudvar*

AJKA KRISTÁLY **(117 E3)** (*D10*)

The traditional art of glass-making is still kept alive by some glass-blowing factories in Hungary. One of them is Ajka in western Hungary. In addition to Ajka glass you can buy Zsolnay porcelain here. *V, Kossuth Lajos utca 10 | ajka-crystal.hu | underground 3: Ferenciek tere*

HEREND PORCELAIN ★
(116 C1) *(ⓜ D8)*
This traditional porcelain was already chosen by Queen Victoria for royal use at the World Fair of 1896. Under its owner Mór Fischer, who started making porcelain in 1839, the factory, founded in 1826, achieved global fame. *VI, Andrássy út 16 | www.herend.com | underground 1: Opera*

SHOES

TISZA CIPŐ (117 E2) *(ⓜ E10)*
This Communist era brand has managed to achieve cult status. Young Hungarians are discovering these shoes with the stylized 'T' as a cool alternative to conventional labels. Sportswear too. *VII, Károly körút 1 | www.tiszacipo.hu | underground 2: Astoria*

VASS (117 D3) *(ⓜ D10)*
Vass is an institution! The hand-made shoes from this traditional workshop are equal to any made-to-measure items from London or Munich. The shop sells ready-to-wear shoes for men and women, or you can have your measurements taken for your own last. *V, Haris köz 2 | www.vass-cipo.hu | underground 3: Ferenciek tere*

WINE & PÁLINKA

BORTÁRSASÁG (123 D4) *(ⓜ C8)*
Top-quality wine shop near the Parliament Building. *V, Vécsey utca 5/corner Vértanúk tere | www.bortarsasag.hu | underground 2: Kossuth Lajos tér*

ROYAL WINE MUSEUM
(KIRÁLY BORHÁZ) (119 D5) *(ⓜ B9)*
This wine cellar consists of 13 themed rooms all about wine, including a Champagne room and a pálinka room. There is also a wine shop. You can visit it as part of a guided tour. *Oct–April closed Mon | I, Szent György tér (opposite Café Korona) | www.kiralyiborok.com | bus 16 (castle bus/Várbusz)*

A classic: Herend Porcelain

PÁLINKA HOUSE (117 F2) *(ⓜ E10)*
Hungarian fruit brandies *(pálinka)* have won several awards at the top European fair, the Destillata in Austria. Products from the top distilleries can be found in the Pálinka House. At the beginning of May there is a *Pálinka Festival (www.budapestipalinkafesztival.hu)* in Budapest. *VIII, Rákóczi út 17 | www.magyarpalinkahaza.hu | underground 2: Astoria, buses 173, 178*

ENTERTAINMENT

CITY **WHERE TO START?**

Liszt Ferenc tér is the main destination for Budapest's scene and especially so during the summer months. A second popular street for evening entertainment is **Ráday utca** with its colourful choices of venues and activities; successful young people meet in places such as the Soul Café. An evening stroll through the **Jewish Quarter** will lead you to alternative venues, such as Szimpla beer garden and Szóda. On warm summer nights the people of Budapest go down to the **Danube**. The top venues on the Buda side of the river are Zöld Pardon and the A38 club boat.

What are you in the mood for? Visitors to Budapest will find that the city has a diverse evening programme to offer. Among the wealth of choices are operettas as well as classical music concerts and a vibrant young music scene.

Hungary's music scene is still profiting from the influence of the great musical masters Zoltán Kodály and Béla Bartók, who made a name for themselves both through their compositions and through their commitment to musical education. It's not just fans of classical music who are well catered for. Budapest has a thriving jazz scene, found in clubs and on boats. Young people are particularly attracted to the music cafés and clubs that play funk, house and pop, and also host party events. During the summer open-

Forays among Béla Bartók's heirs: Budapest's operas, concerts and operettas are no less outstanding than the city's pubs and clubs

air clubs and courtyard bars are popular, but many young people in Budapest are also very into traditional folk music.

The people of Budapest love going to the theatre, but for tourists there is language barrier to contend with. For that reason a visit to the opera is a must, for the fantastic ambience alone. Musicals have their firm place and the good old operetta has also been able to assert itself successfully in the home of Franz Léhar and Imre Kálmán. The modern cinemas are particularly popular among teenagers and students. Current international releases are usually shown in the original language (with Hungarian subtitles). Budapest's nightlife also includes revues and everything that falls into the 'red light' category. Like everywhere in the world, utmost care should be taken in the 'red light district'.

A calendar of events can be found in the weekly papers. A comprehensive list can be found on *www.kulturinfo.hu*.

The Szimpla kert beer garden is a popular meeting place during the summer months

BARS & PUBS

ABSZINT (123 E5) (*M E8*)

The café and restaurant celebrates absinthe culture to perfection. The intoxicating drink, made of wormwood, fennel and aniseed, enjoys a cult status among the generally younger clientele. *Daily 11am–11.30pm | VI, Andrássy út 34 | www.abszint.hu | underground 1: Opera*

INSIDERTIP ANDANTE BORPATIKA
(119 E3–4) (*M C9*)

Zsold Tiffán, a top winegrower from Villány, is a co-owner of this wine oasis on the Buda side of the Danube near the Chain Bridge. A selection of four wines served with a ham and salami platter or with goat's cheese is a great option for a sundowner. With such expert advice, and the good food, a first round quickly turns into a second. *Tue–Sat from 4pm |*

I, Bem rakpart 2 | tel. 1 457 08 07 | www.andante-borpatika.hu | buses 16, 105

BAROKKO MUSIC CLUB
(123 F4) (*M E8*)

This club is located in the basement of the café restaurant Barokko. Bands and DJs perform here. There is many a great night to be had in this hip spot. Upstairs the Barokko has a bar that serves 75 different cocktails. It's not easy to get a seat outside during the summer months. *Thu, Fri, Sat from 5pm | VI, Liszt Ferenc tér 5 | tel. 1 322 07 00 | www.barokko.hu | underground 1: Oktogon*

BECKETT'S (123 E4) (*M D7*)

The Irish bar, with its restaurant and summer terrace, is one of the city's most popular meeting places, particularly for businesspeople living in Budapest. You will hear more English than Hungarian here. *Daily, Bar/Pub from noon | V, Bajcsy Zsilinszky út 72 | www.becketts.hu | underground 3: Arany János utca*

INSIDER TIP ▶ **CSENDES BAR**
(117 E3) (*□ E10*)
This bar demonstrates just how young and hip a fine period property can be. The creative interior has a wonderfully relaxing atmosphere, particularly in the evenings. This bar only serves snacks to eat. Among the largely younger clientele are Budapest's creative scene and students from the nearby university. *Mon–Fri from 8am, Sat from 2pm, Sun from 4pm | V, Ferenczy István utca 7 | underground 2: Astoria*

DOMUS VINORUM (123 E5) (*□ D9*)
The complex cellar near St Stephen's Basilica is both pleasant and quite cool (in the literal sense). The vaulted rooms contain more than 30,000 bottles of wine. You can get in the mood for the rest of the evening by tasting some wines along with tasty treats such as *kolbász* (winter sausage), salami or cheese. *Daily 10am–8pm | V, Bajcsy-Zsilinszky út 18 | www.domusvinorum.hu | underground 1: Bajcsy-Zsilinszky út*

INSTANT BAR (123 E4) (*□ E8*)
The building and courtyard once stood abandoned, now they are busier than ever and a bit strange too: there is one room where tables and chairs are dangling from the ceiling, while a school of fish are suspended above the guests' heads in the courtyard. The cellar hosts long party nights with DJs and bands. *Daily from 4pm | VI, Nagymező utca 38 | underground 1: Oktogon*

JANIS' PUB (117 E4) (*□ E10*)
A cosy Irish pub, with live music. *Mon–Sat from 4pm | V, Király Pál utca 8 | www.janispub.hu | underground 3: Kálvin tér*

SZIMPLA
In summer *Szimpla kert (daily from noon)*, the beer garden, is a cool location. Crumbling walls surround a courtyard popular among the city's younger crowd. Open all year round are *Café Szimpla (Mon–Fri 10am–noon)* and *Restaurant Dupla (daily)*. *Beer garden: VII, Kazinczy utca 14 | underground 2: Astoria* (123 F6) (*□ E8*) | *café, restaurant: VII, Kertész utca 48 | trams 4, 6* (123 F5) (*□ E8*) | *www.szimpla.hu*

INSIDER TIP ▶ **SZÓDA** (123 F6) (*□ E9*)
A café bar near the Great Synagogue that's very popular with young Hungarians. People meet upstairs for a drink, to nibble popcorn or to eat a sandwich. Soda from the siphon is free. Downstairs there's a dance floor for parties that start late in the evening at weekends. *Daily from 9am | II, Wesselényi utca 18 | www.szoda.com | underground 2: Astoria*

MARCO POLO HIGHLIGHTS

★ **Béla Bartók Concert Hall**
The top address for classical concerts in the Palace of Arts
→ p. 78

★ **Danube Palace**
The stage for the major folk ensembles → p. 78

★ **Liszt Ferenc Academy of Music**
A harmony of architecture and music → p. 78

★ **Hungarian State Opera House**
Pomp and magnificence of the musical theatre with a look behind the scenes → p. 79

CASINO

CASINO

VÁRKERT CASINO (119 E5) *(ᗅ C10)*
Situated in the historic ambience of the former waterworks in Buda Castle. The city's most-visited casino, with its own jetty on the Danube. *Daily round the clock | I, Ybl Miklós tér 9 | bus 86*

CINEMAS

MŰVÉSZ, URÁNIA, PUSKIN
These three are the classic, completely restored old picture palaces. They mainly show art-house movies (no action films). *Művész: VI, Teréz körút 30 | underground 3: Nyugati pályaudvar* (123 E4) *(ᗅ E8) | Uránia: VII, Rákóczi út 25 | underground 2: Blaha Lujza tér, bus 7* (124 A6) *(ᗅ F9) | Puskin: V, Kossuth Lajos utca 18 | underground 3: Ferenciek tere* (117 E3) *(ᗅ D10)*

PALACE CINEMAS
The popular multiplex cinemas are the attraction in the large shopping and recreational centres Westend City Center and MOM Park. *Westend City Center: VI, Váci út 1–3 (near the Western Station) | underground 3: Nyugati pályaudvar* (123 E2–3) *(ᗅ E6–7) | MOM Park: XII., Corner of Alkotás út/Csörsz utca | tram 6* (126 A2) *(ᗅ A10) | www.palacecinemas.hu*

CONCERTS, OPERAS & OPERETTAS

BÉLA BARTÓK CONCERT HALL (BARTÓK BÉLA NEMZETI HANGVERSE-NYTEREM) ★ ● (128 A6) *(ᗅ F14)*
The 'National Béla Bartók Concert Hall', with its 1,700 seats, is the core of the Palace of Arts. Its acoustics are a marvel of modern engineering. This concert hall sees performances by the Hungarian National Philharmonic Orchestra as well as major orchestras and soloists from around the world. *IX, Komor Marcelli utca 1 | www.mupa.hu | trams 12, 2A*

DANUBE PALACE (DUNA PALOTA) ★ (116 C1) *(ᗅ C9)*
This Neo-baroque music hall hosts concerts by the Danube Symphony Orchestra, which mainly plays popular pieces, e.g. by Lehár, Brahms, Liszt, Strauss, Kálmán and Haydn. The well-known *Danube Folk Ensemble* and *Rajkó Folk Ensemble* also perform here. *V, Zrínyi utca 5 | tel. 1 2 35 55 01 | www.duna palota.hu | buses 15, 115*

FRANZ LISZT ACADEMY OF MUSIC (ZENEAKADÉMIA) ★ (123 F4–5) *(ᗅ E8)*
This academy, built between 1904 and 1907, is Hungary's most important conservatoire. It has two concert halls in which classical concerts are performed. The large hall is an Art Nouveau masterpiece. Even if you're not going to attend a concert, you should take a look at the foyer to enjoy the outstanding Art Nouveau style. There are plans to have the academy comprehensively renovated. *VI, Liszt Ferenc tér 8 | tel. 1 3 42 01 79 | underground 1: Oktogon, trams 4, 6*

COMEDY THEATRE OF BUDAPEST (VÍGSZÍNHÁZ) (123 D3) (*D7*)

The theatre, opened in 1896, is a riot architectural eclecticism. Performances include classics such as Arthur Miller, William Shakespeare and Friedrich Dürrenmatt. There are also other good productions you can go and see for which you do not need to understand Hungarian, such as 'The Jungle Book'. No performances June–Sept | *XIII, Szent István körút 14 | tel. 1 3 40 46 50 | www.vigszin haz.hu | trams 2, 4, 6*

MADÁCH THEATRE (MADÁCH SZÍNHÁZ) (124 A5) (*F9*)

This theatre was the first to get the right to stage an Andrew Lloyd Webber musical according to its own ideas. The 'Phantom of the Opera' was a great success. It was followed by the rock musical 'Jesus Christ Superstar'. *Closed Aug | VII, Erzsébet körút 29–33 | tel. 1 4 78 20 41 | www.madach szinhaz.hu | trams 4, 6*

HUNGARIAN STATE OPERA HOUSE (OPERAHÁZ) ★ (123 E5) (*D–E8*)

Accompanying the great artistry on the programme is the visual pleasure of the surroundings. During an interval, standing on one of the balconies that look out on Andrássy út is a special experience. The opera house can be visited daily at 3pm or 4pm; tickets are available from the shop (at the side, in Hajós utca). *VI, Andrássy út 20 | tel. 1 3 32 79 14 | www. opera.hu | underground 1: Opera*

INSIDER TIP OPERETTA SHIP (OPERETTHAJÓ) (123 D6) (*C9–10*)

Artists from the opera house and the operetta and musical theatre perform during an atmospheric, two-hour evening boat trip (with or without food; from the jetty in Vigadó tér). *15 April–31 Oct*

Wed, Fri, Sun 8pm | Tickets online, in hotels and ticket agencies | tel. 1 4 02 00 63 | www.operetthajo.hu

Hi-tech for sound: the Bélá Bartók Concert Hall

BUDAPEST OPERETTA AND MUSICAL THEATRE (OPERETT-SZÍNHÁZ) (123 E4) (*E8*)

It is not just the theatre that has been renovated. The performances are better than ever too. Outstanding performers and modern productions even portray classics such as 'Countess Maritza' in a new light. Also part of the repertoire are musicals such as 'West Side Story'. *VI, Nagymező utca 19 | tel. 1 3 53 21 72 | www.operettszinhaz.hu | bus 178*

PEST REDOUBT (PESTI VIGADÓ) (116 C2) (*C–D9*)

With its renovation, this long-established temple of the arts (operettas, concerts) has become a stunningly beautiful venue on the banks of the Danube. *V, Vigadó tér*

Crossover on the Danube: the A38 club boat complete with restaurant and rock music

2 | www.pestivigado.hu | underground 1: Vörösmarty tér

MUSIC CLUBS

A38 (127 F5) (*💯 F13*)

Welcome aboard! The A38 is said to be one of Budapest's coolest music venues, and you can spend a great evening here with a restaurant on the upper deck and performance space below. Among the diverse musical offerings are performances by bands from eastern Europe, often a crossover of rock, jazz and folk. *Daily | XI, on the Buda side not far from Pefőfi Bridge | www.A38.hu | trams 4, 6*

BUDAPEST JAZZ CLUB (117 F4) (*💯 E10*)

Top-quality jazz performances held in an elegant two-storey villa with modern engineering for optimum sound. Hungarian jazz stars such as Veronika Harcsa and the *Grenscó Kollektiv* perform here. It is worth keeping an eye out for the programmes, such as for jam sessions (after 11pm) and Sunday concerts. Includes a jazz café. Tickets and information also available from *Ticket Express* and *www.jegymester.hu*. *VIII, Múzeum utca 7 | www.bjc.hu | underground 3: Kálvin tér*

INSIDER TIP ▶ CORVINTETŐ ☼

(124 A6) (*💯 F9*)

A cool club on the roof of the Corvin department store, which really buzzes in the early hours of the morning. A 30-metre bar, a dance floor, electronic music and swing seats outside, everything illuminated in red light. The entrance is a nondescript door covered in graffiti in Somogyi Béla utca. Anyone wanting to enjoy the view in peace and quiet should come up here for drinks in the early evening. *Spring to autumn daily from 6pm | IX, Blaha Lujza tér 1–2 | www.corvinteto.hu | underground 2: Blaha Lujza tér*

HOLDUDVAR (122 C1) (*💯 C5*)

The party crowds set the tone on Margaret Island during the summer months. Behind the fountain (to the right of the main road) is Holdudvar, which is firmly in the hands of young party-goers on weekend nights. This place also has table-football and table-tennis. Otherwise the elegant neoclassical building (formerly a casino) is a normal café restaurant. *Closed Oct–April | XIII, Margaret Island | www.holdudvar.net | trams 4, 6 and bus 26*

JAZZYPUB (123 F4) (*💯 E8*)

The Jazzypub, the club of the Jazzy radio station, is based at Café Mediterrán.

Highlights include the 'Jazzpub' evenings on Thu, Fri and Sat *VI, Liszt Ferenc tér 10 | www.jazzypub.hu | underground 1: Oktogon*

OLD MAN'S MUSIC PUB
(123 F5) (*[]] F9*)

Every evening from 9pm onwards bands play jazz, soul, funk, country, blues or swing here. A relaxed atmosphere and good food (daily 3pm–4am). *VII, Akácfa utca 13 | www.oldmansmusicpub.com | underground 2: Blaha Lujza tér*

SYMBOL (120 A5) (*[]] B6*)

The 1780 building has become a cool, multifaceted location. There is a café, an Italian restaurant, *Puskas-Sport-Pub* with live broadcasts, a gallery, the *Live Music Club* and a garden. It gets particularly busy during summer weekends. On the Buda side between Margaret Island and Árpád Bridge. *III, Bécsi út 56 | www.symbolbudapest.hu | buses 86, 60, 6, tram 17 (from Margaret Bridge)*

INSIDER TIP SIRÁLY (123 F5) (*[]] E9*)

Anyone wanting a coffee or a beer while getting a taste of a young, creative scene should go to the 'Seagull' in the trendy Király utca. Exhibitions are held upstairs, while a multicultural art scene meets downstairs in a relaxed atmosphere. There is even some Hebrew rap. *Mon–Fri from 10am, Sat, Sun from 11am | VI, Király utca 50 | www.siraly.co.hu | underground 1: Opera, trams 4, 6*

TAKE 5 (117 D1) (*[]] D9*)

Enter through a dark door and go down the stairs. Once you're actually there, spirits will rise: traditional jazz, fusion, soul and funk are performed by international and Hungarian artists. If you have an appetite for more than just music, you can also eat here. *Wed–Sun 6pm–2am |* *VI, Paulay Ede utca 2 (cellar of the Vista travel agent) | www.take5.hu | underground 1: Bajcsy-Zslinszky ú*

DANCE & FOLKLORE

BUDA REDOUTE (BUDAI VIGADÓ)
(119 D2) (*[]] B8*)

The internationally renowned *Danube Folk Ensemble* is just one of the troupes that performs folk dance and music here. *I, Corvin tér 8 | www.ticket.info.hu | bus 86*

FONÓ (FONÓ BUDAI ZENEHÁZ) (0) (*[]] C15*)

The Fonó Music House in Buda has a comprehensive, colourful culture and entertainment programme and is extremely popular with the people of Budapest. Folk-music bands also regularly perform here. Away from the city centre, south of Lagymányosi Bridge. *IX, Sztregova utca 3 | www.fono.hu | trams 41, 47*

NATIONAL DANCE THEATRE (NEMZETI TANC SZÍNHÁZ) (122 B5) (*[]] B9*)

National and international ballet companies perform here. The dance theatre has another performance venue in the theatre space in the Palace of Arts. Several bars and the generous space make even the interval an enjoyable experience. *I, Színház utca 1–3 | www.nemzetitancszinhaz.hu | bus 16 (castle bus/Várbusz)*

INSIDER TIP RAM COLOSSEUM
(120 C6) (*[]] D5*)

With this theatre and event complex in Pest (opposite Margaret Island) Budapest has acquired another attractive cultural venue. Among the artists performing here is the dance group Experidance *(www.experidance.hu)* with their fantastic, colourful shows. *VIII, Kárpát utca 23–25 | www.ramcolosseum.hu | underground 3: Dózsa György út*

WHERE TO STAY

Budapest can measure up to any other city when it comes to top-quality four and five-star accommodation. The number of luxury hotels is rising year by year and they're always at full capacity.

The main reason for this is that Budapest is the country's economic centre and an important conference location. Visitors who want a first-class experience, but not at sky-high prices, will mainly be interested in the weekend rates and the packages offered by the leading hotels. The trend for more comfort is also taking place in the mid-price range. Very basic hotels have all but disappeared, because there's hardly any demand anymore.

The dividing line in the less expensive section runs between three-star hotels and guesthouses. Inexpensive accommodation is available in hostels *(www.hostels.hu)*, whose fittings are correspondingly basic, and in student residences (in July and August), whose standard may leave some something to be desired.

Booking hotels directly in Budapest is significantly more expensive than doing it online. Those who do a thorough search will find deals for quite a few expensive hotels outside the main season, such as for 95 euros instead of 200.

Special offers can be found on sites such as *www.budapesthotelreservation.com*, *www.budapesthotelstart.com* and *www.budapesthotels.com*.

Photo: Hotel Gellért and Liberty Bridge

Sleep well: first-class hotels are booming, and there's a trend for a lot more comfort quite generally too

DANUBIUS HOTEL ASTORIA
(117 E3) *(ΩΩ E10)*

This long-established hotel was based on the New York Waldorf Astoria. It never was quite so luxurious and it still isn't, but a recent revamp has given its historic charm a new lustre. Pure nostalgia can be felt in the Belle Époque ambience of the café restaurant *Mirror*. *130 rooms | V, Kossuth Lajos utca 19–21 | tel.* *1 88 96 00 | www.danubiushotels.com/ astoria | underground 2: Astoria*

BUDA CASTLE FASHION HOTEL
(118 B2) *(ΩΩ A8)*

This small luxury oasis on Castle Hill is a real jewel. The hotel is not far from Matthias Church and blends in perfectly with the historical surroundings. All the rooms are non-smoking. *25 rooms | I, Úri utca 39 | tel. 1 2 24 79 00 | www. budacastlehotelbudapest.com | buses*

The Fisherman's Bastion reflected in the façade of the Hilton

16, 16 A from Széll Kálmán tér (formerly Moszkva tér)

DANUBIUS HOTEL GELLÉRT
(127 D3) (*m* D11)

This building is a fabulous example of Art Nouveau, built in 1918. But when it comes to décor and service, it is not quite up to the same standards as other hotels in this category. Spa and wellness guests appreciate its proximity to the Gellért Spa and Baths. The brasserie, with its terrace (views of the Danube), is also a popular spot for non-residents. *234 rooms | XI, Szent Gellért tér 1 | tel. 1 8 89 55 00 | www.danubiushotels.com/gellert | tram 49*

HILTON BUDAPEST (118 C2) (*m* B8)

This hotel is fascinating because of its location on Castle Hill and the incorporation of historical elements into the design. For example, you can see parts of a church nave and the tower of St Nicholas. *322 rooms | I, Hess András tér 1–3 | tel. 1 8 89 66 00 | www.budapest.hilton.com | bus 16 (castle bus/Várbusz)*

LÁNCHÍD 19 ★ (116 A1–2) (*m* C9)

This temple of design near the Chain Bridge is an architectural tribute to glass as a building material. The interior design is inspired by the likes of Alvar Aalto as well as incorporating features specially created for this hotel. The foyer has a glass floor that reveals views of Roman ruins below. *47 rooms | I, Lanchíd utca 19 | tel. 1 4 19 19 00 | www.lanchid19hotel.hu | bus 86*

DANUBIUS HEALTH SPA RESORT
MARGITSZIGET (120 C4) (*m* D3)

With its superb facilities, the former Margitsziget spa hotel on peaceful Margaret Island has emerged as a stunning oasis of relaxation. At its core are its modern pools and thermal baths, as well as numerous wellness therapies and beauty treatments. *267 rooms | tel. 1 8 89 47 00 | www.danubiushotels.com/margitsziget | bus 26*

MARRIOTT BUDAPEST (116 C3) (*m* D10)

This establishment keeps winning awards as a popular business hotel. And with its ten storeys it cannot be beaten when it comes to location either: all the rooms have views of the Danube. *362 rooms | V, Apáczai Csere J. utca 4 | tel. 1 4 86 50 00 | www.marriott.com | underground 1: Vörösmarty tér, tram 2*

HOTELS: MODERATE

ADINA APARTMENT HOTEL
(123 E1) (*D6*)

The Adnia combines the freedom of self-catering apartments with hotel service. It has 97 apartments and studios with one or two bedrooms, a wellness centre with an indoor pool, and a breakfast room. *III, Hegedűs Gyula utca 52–54 | tel. 1 2 36 88 88 | www.adina.eu | underground 3: Lehel tér*

INSIDER TIP AMBRA (123 F5) (*E9*)

A smart little hotel just off the newly trendy Király utca. The rooms are a fine mix of comfort and contemporary design. This hotel also has apartments and hypoallergenic rooms. *37 rooms | VII, Kisdiófa utca 13 | tel. 1 3 21 15 33 | www.hotelambra.hu | underground 1: Opera*

ATRIUM HOTEL (124 B6) (*F9*)

The architecture and design of this hotel create a bright atmosphere that is flooded with light. A lot of white and lovely shades of turquoise, blue and yellow give it an elegant, cheerful feel. *72 rooms | VIII, Csokonai utca 14 | tel. 1 2 99 07 77 | www.atriumhotelbudapest.com | underground 2: Blaha Lujza tér*

CONTINENTAL HOTEL ZARA ★
(124 A6) (*E9*)

The inscription above the entrance does not give the hotel's name, instead it says *Hungária Fürdő*. That is a requirement because it is a heritage building and this hotel was once the magnificent Hungária Bath, built in 1827. It is situated in the Jewish Quarter and was faithfully re-

stored in 2010, turning it into a modern and comfortable hotel. The lobby alone is a feast for the eyes. There are two inviting courtyards and a roof garden with a large wellness area. *272 rooms | VII, Dohány utca 42–44 | tel. 1 8 15 10 10 | www.continentalhotelzara.com | underground 2: Blaha Lujza tér*

ERZSÉBET (117 E4) (*D10*)

This hotel, opened in 1873, has a perfect city-centre location and has been completely modernised, from the rooms' interiors to the technology. Guests will find an upscale three-star establishment. *123 rooms | V, Károlyi Mihály utca 11–15 | tel. 1 8 89 37 00 | www.danubiushotels.com/erzsebet | underground 3: Ferenciek tere*

MARCO POLO HIGHLIGHTS

★ **Lánchíd 19**
Designer highlight with an unusual glass façade → p. 84

★ **Continental Hotel Zara**
A luxury oasis in the former Hungária Bath dating from 1827 → p. 85

★ **Corinthia Grand Hotel Royal**
Long-established grand hotel on the Ring → p. 86

★ **Four Seasons Gresham Palace**
This luxury hotel near the Danube is a magnificent Art Nouveau building with a stunningly beautiful interior → p. 86

★ **Ibis Centrum**
The hotel has a great city location and good prices, as well as pleasant atmosphere and friendly service → p. 89

HOTELS: MODERATE

K + K HOTEL OPERA (123 E5) *(⌕ D8)*
It's the big names who've inspired the design here, such as Le Corbusier, Eileen Gray, Charles Eames, Philippe Starck. Service and atmosphere deserve top marks. The bistro bar is a popular meeting place. *206 rooms | VI, Révay utca 24 | tel. 1 2 69 02 22 | www.kkhotels.com | underground 1: Opera*

MAMAISON RESIDENCE IZABELLA (123 F4) *(⌕ E7)*
Many of the generously sized (45 to 97 sq m) feel-good apartments, which are even decked out with wooden floors, look out onto the pretty courtyard and have a balcony. The hotel has a sauna and a gym. The inviting 19th-century building is not far from Andrássy út boulevard. *38 suites | VI, Izabella utca 61 | tel. 1 4 75 59 00 | www.mamaison.com | underground 1: Vörösmarty tér*

MERCURE KORONA (117 E4) *(⌕ E10)*
Favourably located (for transport) on the Small Boulevard (Kiskörút), this hotel, with comparatively small rooms, benefits from the lively atmosphere of its surroundings. *424 rooms | V, Kecskeméti utca 14 | tel. 1 4 86 88 00 | www.mercure-korona.hu | underground 3: Kálvin tér, trams 47, 49*

INSIDER TIP ▶ SOHO BOUTIQUE HOTEL (124 A5) *(⌕ F9)*
The blue, yellow and orange façade lighting is a clear signal in the evenings that the Soho has brought a touch of

LUXURY HOTELS

Corinthia Grand Hotel Royal ★ (123 F5) *(⌕ E8)*
The old Grand Hotel Royal has been reopened in all its former glory. A nice place for a coffee is the Brasserie Royal in the atrium. *441 rooms | from 140 euros | VII. Erzsébet körút 43–49 | tel. 1 4 79 40 00 | www.corinthiahotels.com | underground 1: Oktogon, trams 4, 6*

Four Seasons Gresham Palace ★ (116 B1) *(⌕ C9)*
Top-class Art Nouveau splendour can be found in this hotel by the Chain Bridge. The wonderful interior can also be enjoyed during a lunch or in the ● café, where you can sample some delicious cakes. *169 rooms | from 250 euros | V., Széchenyi István tér 5–6 | tel. 1 2 68 60 00 | www.fourseasons.com/budapest | underground 1: Vörösmarty tér, tram 2*

Le Meridien (117 D1) *(⌕ D9)*
The style of this grand hotel is classic elegance, from the lobby with its fireplace to the Le Bourbon restaurant with its Art-deco dome and the health club, which features a pool with a glass roof. *218 rooms | from 140 euros | V. Erzsébet tér 9–10 | tel. 1 4 29 55 00 | www.starwoodhotels.com | underground 1, 2, 3: Deák Ferenc tér*

New York Palace Budapest (124 A–B6) *(⌕ F9)*
This magnificent building with its tower is an eye-catcher. The owners of the imposing five-star temple have delivered what they promised: it is an 'ambassador of the Italian lifestyle'. *107 rooms | from 180 euros | VII., Erszébet körút 9–11 | tel. 1 8 86 61 11 | www.boscolohotels.com | underground 2: Blaha Lujza tér*

A shining beacon of Art Nouveau: the interior of the Gresham Palace Hotel

avant-garde into Dóhany utca. Retro colours and design also set the tone in the lobby bar. The rooms are painted in more muted tones and are very comfortable and well equipped. *74 rooms | VII, Dohány utca 64 | tel. 1 8 72 82 92 | www.sohoboutiquehotel.com | underground 2: Baha Lujza tér, trams 4, 6*

SPINOZA (123 E6) (𝖔 E9)

Those who like to be at the heart of things, and in this case in the up-and-coming Jewish Quarter, will feel right at home in the Spinoza restaurant and theatre. There are four apartments for guests on the 1st and 2nd floors (no lift). The atmosphere is casual and friendly. There are various sizes of apartments, including one with three rooms and a gallery. *VI, Dob utca 15 | tel. 1 4 13 74 88 | www.spinozahaz.hu | underground 1: Astoria*

HOTEL: BUDGET & GUESTHOUSES

BAROSS (124 C5) (𝖔 G9)

Behind the inconspicuous entrance (near the Eastern Station) there is a wonderful Art Nouveau ensemble, situated around a courtyard. The best view of it is from the panoramic lift, which goes up to the guesthouse on the 5th floor. The establishment is very comfortable, is good value for money and has a very clean, friendly ambience. *45 rooms | VII, Baross tér 15 | tel. 1 4 61 30 10 | www.barosshotel.hu | underground 2: Keleti pályaudvar*

INSIDER TIP ► CENTRAL BASILICA (123 D5) (𝖔 D9)

Both the location and the room prices are excellent. Situated right by St Stephen's Basilica (on the car-free forecourt of the magnificent church), this hotel has the best three-star levels of comfort. *46 rooms (non-smoking) | V, Hercegprimás utca 8 | tel. 1 3 28 50 10 | www.hotel centralbasilica.hu | underground 1: Bajcsy-Zsilinszky út*

tively small and basic, but also inexpensive. That's the concept of the Easy chain. Can only be booked online. *59 rooms | VI, Eötvös utca 25/a | www.easyhotel.com | underground 1: Oktogon*

The hotel's name is self-explanatory, given this outstanding location: Central Basilica

CITY HOTEL MÁTYÁS (117 D4) (*⚡ D10*)

Breakfast is served in the famous *Matthias Cellar* with its lavish decor. The hotel is situated above the long-established restaurant. The Váci utca shopping street is only 50 metres away. *85 rooms | V, Március 15. tér 7 | tel. 1 3 18 05 95 | www. cityhotelmatyas.hu | underground 3: Ferenciek tere*

EASYHOTEL (123 F3–4) (*⚡ E7*)

This hotel is only a ten-minute walk from the sophisticated Andrássy út. There's no service here and the rooms are rela-

INSIDER TIP FORTUNA HOTEL SHIP (123 D1–2) (*⚡ D5–6*)

Enjoying the Danube close up while having breakfast on the terrace in the morning: this is possible on the *Fortuna*. The boat is located on the Pest side of the city opposite Margaret Island. The hotel rooms (on the upper deck) have good three-star comfort levels. The best rooms are the four ✻ superior rooms, which also have stunning views. There is an inexpensive hostel with 14 rooms downstairs. *56 rooms (non-smoking) | III, Szent István Park, Alsó rakpart | tel.*

1 2 88 81 00 | www.fortunahajo.hu | trams 2, 4, 6, bus 75, 76

IBIS CENTRUM ★ (117 F5) *(🛒 E11)*

The service and the entire ambience of this hotel in the Ráday utca pedestrian zone is very friendly. It's also excellent value for money. *126 rooms | IX, Ráday utca 6 | tel. 1 456 41 00 | www.ibis-centrum.hu | underground 3: Kálvin tér*

INSIDER TIP PEST (123 E5) *(🛒 E8)*

The architects and owners have turned one of the oldest buildings in this part of town into a real gem. They integrated part of the old masonry into the building and also restored the beautiful old courtyard. A further plus is its location close to Andrássy út. *25 rooms | VI, Paulay Ede utca 31 | tel. 1 343 11 98 | www.hotelpest.hu | underground 1: Opera*

INSIDER TIP STAR (124 C4) *(🛒 G8)*

The neighbourhood is still fairly dull, but the hotel itself has been completely renovated inside and out. It has a young, fresh atmosphere and also has family rooms (rooms with connecting doors). The central location and the fair prices are further benefits. *48 rooms | VII, István utca 14 | tel. 1 479 04 20 | www.starhotel.hu | underground 2: Keleti Pályaudvar, bus 74, 79*

HOTEL VADVIRÁG PENSION (O) *(🛒 0)*

These two beautiful villas in Buda, with views over the city, are done out in period furnishings and décor (velvet coverings, settees etc.). Some rooms have a terrace. *14 rooms | II, Nagybányai út 18 | tel. 1 275 02 00 | www.hotelvadviragpanzio.hu | bus 5 from Széll Kálmán tér (formerly Moszkva tér) to Pasaréti tér, then one stop on bus 29*

HOSTEL

RED BUS HOSTEL (117 E3) *(🛒 D10)*

Centrally located near the synagogue on the 1st floor (ring downstairs). Clean rooms in an old building with high ceilings, breakfast, internet access, kitchen and washing machines. A bunk bed in a four- or six-bed dorm is very inexpensive (approx. 9 euros). A double room costs approx. 35 euros. *V, Semmelweis utca 14 | tel. 1 266 01 36 | www.redbusbudapest.hu | underground 2: Astoria*

LOW BUDGET

▶ Good location, good prices: spaces in Bánki are particularly popular for the Sziget Festival (price per person in a double room 15 euros, during the festival 17 euros). The four floors (in a student hall of residence) are only open in July and August. *31 rooms | VI., Podmaniczky utca 8 | tel. 20 776 22 64 | www.mellowmood.hu | underground 3: Nyu-gati Pályaudvar* (123 E4) *(🛒 D7–8)*

▶ The good location and special discounts make Hotel Medosz interesting (basic, quite small rooms). Students up to the age of 18, accompanying parents, and pensioners get a 10 percent discount; police officers (IPA pass) get 20 percent off. As an example, pensioners pay approx. 54–60 euros in a double room (incl. buffet breakfast). *70 rooms | VI., Jókai tér | tel. 1 374 30 00 | www.medoszhotel.hu | trams 4, 6, underground 1: Oktogon* (123 F4) *(🛒 E8)*

WALKING TOURS

The tours are marked in green in the street atlas,
the pull-out map and on the back cover

1 ROUND TRIP ON CASTLE HILL

Castle Hill rises 60m (almost 200ft) above the banks of the Danube. Despite all the disasters that have struck this historic core of the city, such as earthquakes, fires, sieges and wars, the hill, which is 1.5km (1 mile) long and up to 500m wide, is a gem of cultural history. Two-thirds of the area is taken up by the Castle Quarter, the other third by the enormous Buda Castle itself. Plan to spend three to four hours on this walk.

The nicest way to get up Castle Hill is to take the **Castle Hill Funicular** (Sikló | in even weeks closed on Mon, otherwise daily 7.30am–10.30pm). During the two-minute trip it travels 95m on a 48 percent gradient, from **Clark Ádám tér** (by the Chain Bridge) to **Szent György tér**. Castle Hill is also a residential area, but few people live within the historic walls. Most of the private houses have hardly been modernised. During the summer months Castle Hill fills with visitors, but in winter it is a quiet and in some places looks abandoned. There are plans to revitalise the area, but none have been implemented yet. For visitors this district, with its many attractions, restaurants, cafés and shops, is a must.

From the funicular's top station turn left to **Buda Castle** → **p. 29** with its museums. The famous **Matthias Fountain** is in the western forecourt. Created by the sculptor Alajos Stróbl (1856–1926), and

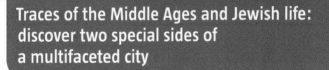

Traces of the Middle Ages and Jewish life: discover two special sides of a multifaceted city

completed in 1904, it recalls the legend of Ilona (according to some sources Ilonka), a peasant girl who encountered the king, Matthias Corvinus, when he was out hunting incognito, and fell in love with him. After she discovered that she had lost her heart to a man who was beyond her reach, she is said to have died of a broken heart. Facing the fountain, you can see her on the left, looking towards the king while protecting her tame fawn from the hunters. The bronze sculpture at the northeastern end

of the palace depicts the **Turul**, a giant mythical bird. According to legend, it is a demigod from whom the Hungarian people are descended.

If you turn right at the hill station, you will reach **Színház utca** (Theatre Street). The neoclassical **Sandor Palace** (Sándor palota), built in 1806, is the official residence of the President of the Republic of Hungary. The palace, no. 1–3, formerly a Carmelite church, was transformed into Buda's first permanent theatre at the behest of Emperor Joseph II; its opening took place in 1790. This **Castle Theatre** (Várszinház) is now home to the National Dance Theatre. During the summer months **Café Rivalda → p. 63** opens up in the pretty courtyard of the monastery. **Dísz tér** (Parade Square) once marked the boundary between the Castle Quarter and the area where the commoners lived. During the Middle Ages executions and markets took place on the square. Continue the walk down **a Tóth Árpád**

The Holy Trinity Column on the square in front of Matthias Church

sétány, a promenade on the defensive walls of Castle Hill with good views of the districts in Buda. Now turn right into **Szentháromság utca** (Holy Trinity Street). Here you will find Buda's **Old Town Hall**, which lost its function when Buda, Óbuda and Pest united in 1873; since then it has been used as a college. The enormous Baroque building runs from **Úri utca** to Szentháromság tér. The tour continues along Úri utca. You will find many relics of the Middle Ages here, such as Gothic seat-alcoves. If you look at the buildings you will see how, after the devastation wrought by the Turks, Baroque buildings were erected on the ruined Gothic ones. The façade of house no. 31 is still Gothic, and there are also still some Gothic elements on houses nos. 32, 34, 36 and 38.

Take the street that runs perpendicular to this one, Dárda utca, to get to **Országház utca** (Parliament Street). There are two fine Gothic buildings here (nos. 18, 20) and a Baroque building (no. 22) that managed to survive the turbulent times. At the end of Országház utca is the pretty **Kapisztrán tér** with the late-Gothic **Mary Magdalene Tower** (Magdolna torony), which plays a carillon every quarter of an hour. Only the tower of the church (13th century) avoided destruction in World War II. The neoclassical **Museum of Military History** (Hadtörténeti Múzeum) was once a barracks. Walk along Petermann biró utca to get to **Bécsi kapu tér** (Vienna Gate Square). On the corner of Fortuna utca is the neoclassical **Protestant church**. It's worth making a short detour to Fortuna utca 4, the new luxury hotel **St George Residence** with its atmospheric courtyard, café and restaurant. The magnificent Baroque building was a museum until its restoration. Now it has been returned to its former glory. The northeastern section of the Castle

Quarter was the Jewish ghetto during the Middle Ages. Its centre, **Táncsics Mihály utca**, was commonly known as 'Jewish Street'. Its most beautiful Baroque building is **Erdődy Palace** (no. 7). The road leads past the hotel to **Matthias Church → p. 33**. The square on which the Hilton is situated is **Hess András tér**. It owes its name to the 15th century German printer, Andreas Hess, who is said to have produced the first book to be printed in Hungary. Matthias Church is located on **Szentháromság tér** (Trinity Square). The 14-m (46ft) **Holy Trinity Column** on the square was set up in 1715 to commemorate the ravages of the plague in 1706.

It is just a few steps from Matthias Church to the **Fisherman's Bastion → p. 30**. The large **equestrian statue** of King Stephen I is another work by sculptor Alajos Stróbl, who allegedly spent ten years working on it in order to get as close to the real person as possible in his depiction. This part of Castle Hill – Matthias Church, Fisherman's Bastion and the equestrian statue – were conceived and implemented by Frigyes Schulek towards the end of the 19th century.

The way back leads along Szentháromság utca and to the left into Úri utca. In building no. 9 you can go down to the **Buda Castle Labyrinth → p. 29**. The fact that the entire Castle Hill has natural caves and tunnels within it has been known since the Middle Ages. You can get back via Úri utca, Dísz tér and the **Royal Stairs** (Kiraly lépcső), which lead to the Danube, or else take the funicular.

2 ERZSÉBETVÁROS: DISCOVERIES IN THE JEWISH QUARTER

Budapest's Zsidónegyed neighbourhood, the Jewish Quarter, has become a very fashionable

Unique: Buda Castle Labyrinth

area. There are places where decay and development are still cheek by jowl, but things are getting more colourful and lively every year. There is plenty of luxury around, as in the fancy hotels and smart shops, restaurants and bars, but there is also young, alternative scene. This walk should take around an hour.

The walk starts at the religious centre of the Jewish community, the **Dohány Street Synagogue → p. 49**, which was ceremonially inaugurated in 1859.

In the early 20th century Budapest was home to around 170,000 Jews. Thanks to the city's tolerance, between 1872 and 1900 the percentage of Jews among the total population had risen from 16 to 21.5 percent. By 1939, an estimated 200,000 Jews lived in the city. Orthodox Jews were always a small minority in Budapest: nothing like a shtetl, a quarter in which the inhabitants lived exclusively reminder of this crime. Today there are around 80,000 Jews in Budapest. Most of them live spread out over the entire city. Erzsébetváros was and is, however, a quarter in which Jewish life has left many marks and in which, first after the end of the horrors of Nazi rule and then

A poignant reminder: the Holocaust Memorial Centre

according to Jewish traditions, ever developed. The vast majority were liberal and to this day consider themselves as part of the Hungarian population.

At the end of 1944, Erzsébetváros, sealed off from the surrounding area by a wall, became a ghetto, and for the Jews confined within it, this became a grave. A total of around 600,000 Hungarian Jews died in the Holocaust. The **Holocaust Memorial Center → p. 50** is a poignant

again after the fall of Communism in 1989, Jewish religion and tradition became a vital force, notwithstanding the fact that the new millennium has seen an unfortunate increase in anti-Semitism in Hungary.

The complete renovation of the Dohány Street Synagogue was made possible by a donation from the American actor Tony Curtis. His father Emanuel Schwartz was a Jewish emigrant from Hungary. The

Jewish Museum → **p. 49** is housed in one of the synagogue's wings.

From the front of the synagogue, follow **Wesselényi utca** along the side of the complex and then turn right to see the **Holocaust Memorial**. Created by the artist Imre Varga, this silvery, shimmering sculpture depicts a weeping willow. It has been placed over mass graves and the names of all the victims are written on the leaves. You can also see **memorial stones** that have been set up in remembrance of the Jews who were murdered or who otherwise died in the ghetto.

If you continue down the road you will pass the modern office building of the accounting and consultancy firm Price-waterhouse Cooper on the corner with Síp utca. At he next junction turn left into Kazinczy utca. This is the location of the **Ministry of Culture** (nos. 24–26), opposite which is the **Electro-technical Museum** (no. 21).

On the corner of **Dob utca** is a piece of history that is not freely accessible: a Jewish school that was closed by the Nazis. Part of the complex has been turned into a synagogue again, used by the city's 3,000 or so Orthodox Jews. Looking left along Dob utca, you will see mostly unrenovated buildings and a number of kosher shops. In the other direction, towards Klauzál tér, more buildings have been renovated.

At Klauzál tér turn left into **Csányi utca** and continue to Király utca. If you take a closer look at the magnificent **corner palace** on the left, which today houses the OTP Bank, you will notice a plaque stating that the former owner, a factory owner, saved more than 100 Jews by hiding them in this building. On the square opposite is the **Terezvaros parish church** built in 1801. The tower was built by architect Miklós Ybl in 1871.

If you now follow **Király utca** in the direction of the river you will find yourself in the middle of a fascinating refurbishment process. In the lower part of the street, towards Deák Ferenc tér, the tone is set by design shops such as **Goa** (no. 21), **Arioso Deko & Café** (no. 9) → **p. 71** and the fancy restaurant bar **Noir et L'Or** (no. 17) → **p. 60**.

After many years of decay, the wonderful complex with the number 13, **Gozsdu Court** → **p. 48**, has been restored to its former glory. Its resurrection as a luxury complex with shops and expensive flats stands in stark contrast to its past. Gozsdu Court was created in the 19th century, after a wealthy philathropist, Emánuel Gozsdu, left a substantial part of his sizeable fortune to the foundation called Fundapiunea lui Gozsdu to support Romanian students of the Greek Orthodox faith pursuing their studies in Hungary. The residence was subsequently constructed, but during World War II terror reigned here. The two entrances were kept closed by force, so that the majority of the inhabitants died of starvation. Now leave Király utca and turn left into **Rumbach utca**. After just a few steps you will have, through an archway on your right, a great view of Buda and the citadel on the hill ✿. The **Rumbach Synagogue** → **p. 49** was designed by Viennese architect Otto Wagner in 1872, in the Romanesque-Moorish style; it is occasionally open. Around 18,000 Jews were imprisoned here in 1944. There is still a lot of work to do in this street. Opposite the shop **La Petite Française** → **p. 71** there is still a derelict site temporarily being used as a car park.

If you finally turn right into Dob utca from Rumbach utca, and then turn left, you will get back to the starting point of this tour.

TRAVEL WITH KIDS

AQUARENA WATER PARK (131 E4) (*🏫 0*)
This aquapark, laid out on terraces, has a lot of watery fun to offer, including 8 pools, 26 flumes and a 'blue cave'. *May–Sept daily 9am–7pm | entry fee 4000 Ft., Children up to the age of 10 2000 Ft., children up to the age of 3 go free | www.aquarena.hu | HÉV from Örs Vezér tér/terminal station underground 2 towards Gödöllő, Station Mogyoród, and from there a bus*

INSIDER TIP ON TOUR WITH A BRINGÓ MOBILE (120 B4) (*🏫 D3*)
You can hire these pedal-powered vehicles on Margaret Island, where parents and children can easily spend an entire day. Bringós can be hired as tandems, for small children or families (four people); electric versions that you don't have to pedal are also available. *Bringóhinto Margit-sziget | Alfréd sétány 1 | www.bringohinto.hu | bus 26, 106 (Árpád Bridge)*

INSIDER TIP KÁROLYI KERT (117 E3–4) (*🏫 E10*)
A well-tended green oasis near the Múzeum körút, surrounded by a wrought iron fence and gates: small but delightful for young and old. Students are absorbed in their books, people chat in the shade of the trees, while others enjoy their lunch in peace and quiet. Part of this garden is a children's playground. *V, Károlyi kert | underground 2: Astoria*

CHILDREN'S RAILWAY (GYERMEKVASÚT) (130 C4–5) (*🏫 0*)
The narrow-gauge railway is operated by children (under supervision). The track through the woods is 11km (7 miles) long. To get here take tram 56 from Széll Kálmán tér (formerly Moszkva tér) to the cog railway station *(Városmajor),* which leads up Széchenyi hegy hill. From here you can walk to the children's railway. Its stations are good starting points for hikes into the Buda Hills. *May–Aug daily. 9am–7pm, Sept–April Tue–Sun 9am–5pm | ticket price 1400 Ft., children 600 Ft. | www.gyermekvasut.hu*

HUNGARIAN NATURAL HISTORY MUSEUM (MAGYAR TERMÉSZETTUDOMÁNYI MÚZEUM) (128 C3) (*🏫 H12*)
The museum is completely tailored to children: there are many interactive games, simulated landscapes with animals and humans, an underwater hall and lots more. The choice is too big rather than too small. *Wed–Mon 10am–6pm | Ticket for all exhibitions 2000 Ft., children 1000 Ft. | VIII, Ludovika tér 2–6 | www.nhmus.hu | underground 3: Klinikák*

Splashing around, being amazed, feeding the goats: from flumes to petting zoos, there's lots to experience for young visitors to Budapest

PALATINUS OPEN-AIR BATH (PALATINUS FÜRDŐ) (120 B4–5) (*ℳ C4*)
This outdoor swimming pool complex (in a large park), with its eleven pools and five slides (four 120m flumes, one kamikaze flume), has lots to keep young and old entertained. During high summer the pools (including a wave pool) tend to be very full. *May–mid-Sept daily 8am–7pm | Entry 2200 Ft., children 1700 Ft. | XIII, Margaret Island | bus 26*

TROPICARIUM (130 C6) (*ℳ O*)
The chief attraction of this 3,000 sq m underwater world are five sharks that swim past the visitors in a tunnel. Apart from huge aquariums in which many plants and animals live, there is also a rainforest inhabited by birds and reptiles. Children are particularly fond of the small monkeys. *Daily 10am–8pm | XXII, in the Campona shopping centre, Nagytétényi út 37–45 | Entry 2300 Ft., children/teens 4–18 years and adults over the age of 62 1600 Ft. | www.tropicarium.hu | buses 3, 14, 114*

VIDÁM PARK (124 C1) (*ℳ G5*)
An amusement park with a historical merry-go-round, a swingboat that goes all the way over, rollercoasters, a ferris wheel, dinosaurs and more. *April–Sept daily 10am–8om, Oct 10am–6pm | Entry 4700 Ft., children (under 1 m free) up to 1.40 m and adults 62 and older 3300 Ft., special attractions cost extra | XIV, Állatkerti körút 14–16 (in the City Park) | www.vidampark.hu | underground 1: Széchenyi fürdő, Trolleybus 72, bus 30 (Hősök tere)*

ZOO (FŐVÁROSI ÁLLAT-ÉS NÖVÉNYKERT) (124 B1–2) (*ℳ F–G 5–6*)
A real hit with young children is the goat enclosure. Children are allowed to stroke and feed them. There are more than 2,000 animals in this zoo. *May–Aug daily 9am–6.30pm, Nov–Jan until 4pm, otherwise until 5.30pm | Entry 1990 Ft., children 2–14 years 1390 Ft., family ticket (2 adults, 3 children) 5700 Ft. | XIV, Állatkerti körút 6–12 (in the City Park) | www.zoobudapest.com | underground 1: Széchenyi fürdő, Trolleybus 72, bus 30 (Hősök tere)*

FESTIVALS & EVENTS

There is just as much to satisfy lovers of classical art as there is to entertain fans of club and café concerts and rock and pop festivals. Street festivals also contribute much to the charm of the capital. *www.festivalcity.hu*

HOLIDAYS

1 Jan. *New Year's Day*; **15 March** *National holiday celebrating the Hungarian Revolution of 1848*; **Easter Monday; 1 May** *Labour Day*; **Whit Monday; 20 Aug.** *Day of St Stephen of Hungary* (national holiday); **23 Oct.** *Day of the Republic, commemorating the 1956 uprising*; **1 Nov.** *All Saints*; **25/26 Dec.** *Christmas*

FESTIVALS

JANUARY
The ▶ *New Year's Gala Concert,* which takes place every year on 1 January, is a top event (no fixed venue). *www.hungariakoncert.hu*

MARCH
▶ ★ *Budapest Spring Festival* with concerts, opera, operetta and theatre performances. This is Hungary's largest art festival, involving the national artist elite as well as international stars of the cultural scene. Includes numerous and music from great classical pieces to jazz and folk. Usually takes place during the second half of the month. *www.festivalcity.hu*

JUNE
In mid-June there is a week-long celebration of the ▶ *Danube Carnival* culminating in the ▶ *Bridge Festival* with the Danube Water Carnival. The celebrations on the banks of the Danube, which are held between the Chain Bridge and Margaret Bridge, culminate in a firework display. *www.dunaart.com*

JULY/AUGUST
▶ *Budafest:* concerts and ballet events, in venues such as the Dominican Court in the Hilton, in St Stephen's Basilica and in the Opera House. July and first half of August. *www.viparts.hu*
▶ *Summer on the Chain Bridge:* Budapest's most beautiful bridge is turned into an entertainment venue at the weekends. *www.festivalcity.hu*
Concerts of organ music specially arranged for this organ (with works by Mozart, Schubert and Liszt) are held in the ▶ *Baroque St Anne's Church.* *www.hungariakoncert.hu*

Enjoy the celebrations: from café concerts to open-air festivals and street parties: there's always something on in Budapest

Until the middle of August
▶ INSIDER TIP concerts are held on the open-air stage of the Zoo (jazz, easy listening) on Wed at 8.30pm. *www.zoo budapest.com*

AUGUST
A huge event with hundreds of thousands of visitors is ▶ *Sziget Festival* on Óbuda Island, north of Margaret Island, which feels a bit like Woodstock. *www. szigetfestival.com*
On 20 Aug., ▶ ★ the *Day of St Stephen of Hungary,* Budapest hosts a street party. Hundreds of thousands of people attend the evening ● firework display.

AUGUST/SEPTEMBER
▶ ● *Jewish Summer Festival* with many international artists and music ranging from classical to jazz and klezmer. Latin rhythms can also be heard here. The concerts in the Dohány Street Synagogue are particularly nice. *www.zsidonyarifesztival. hu*

OCTOBER
▶ *Budapest Autumn Festival:* contemporary art and dance, theatre, film and photographic exhibitions. *www.festival city.hu*
▶ INSIDER TIP *International Harp Festival* one of the best in the world, in the magnificent setting of Gödöllő Palace. *www.kiralyikastely.hu*

DECEMBER
The best Christmas lights can be found near and in Andrássy út, and in Vörösmarty tér there is also a ▶ *Christmas Market* selling arts and crafts.
On 30 December the ▶ *festival concert of the 100-strong Budapest Gypsy Symphony Orchdestra* is held in the Convention Hall (can also be booked with dinner). *www.viparts.hu*
On 31 Dec. a ▶ *New Year's Eve gala* along with a ball is held in the Opera House. *www.viparts.hu*

LINKS, BLOGS, APPS & MORE

LINKS

▶ www.tripadvisor.com/Search-a_lang.de-a_sub-search.Suche-a_where.nav-qbudapest Overview of accommodation, restaurants and attractions with lots of ratings

▶ www.dopplr.com/place/hu/budapest A good insight into the experiences and recommendations of people who have visited Budapest

▶ www.tripwolf.com/en/guide/show/4277/Hungary/Budapest The worldwide travel guide portal has a broad spectrum of categories (including wellness, adventure and nightlife)

▶ www.biziker.com/venues/ Website especially tailored to business travellers with brief information about hotels, convention centres and trade fair venues (type in ‚Budapest' in the search bar)

▶ www.budapesthotelreservation.hu/ Everything at a glance for your hotel reservation

BLOGS & FORUMS

▶ http://jnordmoe.smugmug.com/Travel/Hungary-2008/Budapest/5736004_B6ACG#366777711_Efo6d Many good photos of almost all of the attractions in the city on the Danube

▶ http://fuckyeahhungary.tumblr.com/ Photo blog with old and new pictures, from the Parliament building via faded black-and-white pics to photos of palacsinta – somewhere between artistic pretensions and tourist memories, and not without a few odd gems

▶ http://budapest-ambassador.blogspot.com/ The self-proclaimed Budapest ambassadors share their personal impressions and show their private snapshots

Regardless of whether you are still preparing your trip or already in Budapest: these addresses will provide you with more information, videos and networks to make your holiday even more enjoyable

VIDEOS & STREAMS

▶ http://vimeo.com/9399520 Very high quality atmospheric winter impressions of the city by day and night – good enough to even make you want to go in summer

▶ www.youtube.com/watch?v=Yc7LJy5Ibko The somewhat alternative holiday experience: diving in flooded mines and industrial buildings from the Soviet era. Budapest from below with an exploratory spirit and a grisly atmosphere

▶ http://vimeo.com/14859205 Even though the city is usually only visible in the background, this music video still has nice images of fairly interesting things, and you'll also find out what Hungarian hip-hop sounds like

▶ www.youtube.com/watch?v=p8HA1iAM3jI Line 1 (Földalatti) was opened in 1896. Here you can get an impression of what it's like to ride in the oldest underground on the European mainland

▶ www.youtube.com/watch?v=vD-k81TdOeg All of the attractions of the leisure and amusement park Vidám Park, compactly presented in one clip

APPS

▶ Smart Maps – Budapest A city map for iPhones and iPod Touch

▶ Budapest Travel Guide – Marco Polo Complete city guide for iPhones

NETWORKS

▶ www.couchsurfing.org/mapsurf.html Follow the link and type in 'Budapest, Hungary' where it says 'city'. More than 900 free couches are waiting for visitors, and their owners for new acquaintances

▶ www.facebook.com/visitbudapest The tourism office also has a facebook page: you'll find tips, you can talk to members and it already has more than 5000 friends

▶ www.travbuddy.com/Budapest-travel-partners-994847 You can find travel buddies here who also want to go to Budapest, or you can meet locals who would like to show you around their city

TRAVEL TIPS

ARRIVAL

Hungarian motorways are toll roads. Vignettes *(matrica)* are available for purchase at the border and at service stations. They cost 1,650 Ft for four days, 2,750 Ft for ten days and 4,500 Ft for 31 days. Keep your receipt *(www.autobahn.hu)*. Those arriving from the north or west will enter Budapest via the M1 motorway. It is no fun to be travelling in the city with a car, not least because of the lack of parking spaces. It is advisable to leave your vehicle in the hotel garage.

Train connections have got better and faster. The train journey from London to Budapest takes just 24 hours, by Eurostar to Paris and high-speed TGV from Paris to Munich, then overnight sleeper to Budapest. Or there are connections via Brussels, Cologne & Vienna. *Train information: www.seat61.com | elvira.mav-start.hu. International train information Budapest: tel. 1 4 6155 00*

RESPONSIBLE TRAVEL

It doesn't take a lot to be environmentally friendly whilst travelling. Don't just think about your carbon footprint whilst flying to and from your holiday destination but also about how you can protect nature and culture abroad. As a tourist it is especially important to respect nature, look out for local products, cycle instead of driving, save water and much more. If you would like to find out more about eco-tourism please visit: *www.ecotourism.org*

There are coach connections with many cities in western Europe. The international bus station is *Népliget (IX, Üllői utca 131 | underground 3: Népliget)*.

The standard national airlines such as British Airways and Malév offer several Budapest flight a day. Among the cheaper airlines, there are flights from London and Manchester with *Easyjet (www.easyjet.com) and Jet2 (www.jet2.com)*, as well as from most western European cities. American Airlines operate direct flights from New York.

There are two airports *(www.bud.hu)*: *Ferihegy 1* and *Ferihegy 2* with the terminals 2 A and 2 B (20 and 24km from the centre). The airport used by the cheap airlines is Ferihegy 1. There are bus connections from the airport, as well as a train connection with the Western Station (with the normal trains on the Budapest–Cegléd–Szolnok line).

Another inexpensive way to get into the city is to use the airport shuttles *(tel. 1 2 96 85 55 | www.airportshuttle.hu)* that will drive you to any address in Budapest (one way per person 2,990 Ft.). A taxi into the city will cost between 1,700 and 5,700 Ft, depending on your destination zone.

From April to the end of October hydrofoils operate on the Danube between Vienna and Budapest (journey time 51/2 hrs., one-way ticket approx. 89 euros). *www.mahartpassnave.hu*

CARS

The maximum speed in Hungary in towns and cities is 50kph, outside towns and cities it is 90kph and on motorways 130kph.

From arrival to weather

Outside towns you must have dipped headlights on during the day too. There is a zero-tolerance policy when it comes to drinking and driving and a seatbelt must be worn on every occupied seat. Talking on mobile phones is only permitted with a hands-free set. You must also carry high-visibility jackets (one for every seat in the vehicle).

In the event of a crash where people were injured, the police must be notified. It is also advisable to notify the police if there are accidents involving material damage *(tel. 107)*. If a driver of a vehicle with a Hungarian number plate caused the crash, he / she will have to inform his / her insurance company or *Hungária Biztosító*. If a foreign driver was to blame, the *Hungária Biztosító* must be informed.
– *Hungária Biztosító: I, Galvani út 44 | tel. 1 4 21 14 21 | Mon–Fri 8am–8pm*
– *Breakdown and emergency service: Magyar Autóklub MAK | tel. nationwide 188*
– *Emergency number of the Hungarian automobile club (Yellow Angels/Sárga angyal): tel. 188*
– *International emergency number: tel. 1 3 45 17 44*

CITY TOURS

You can book city tours *(városnézés)* during the day or at night, tours of the Hungarian Parliament Building and trips to Buda Castle in hotels, travel agencies and tourist offices. City tours, some in open buses, are run by *Buda Tours (tel. 1 3 74 70 70 | www.budatours.hu)*. If you take advantage of a *hop-on-hop-off-tour* (red buses) there are 15 different stops where you can get on and off as the mood takes you, such as at the Opera House. *Hop-on-Hop-off* is also available

on the water (but wait for the boat to dock before you hop off!); you can get on at Vigadó tér (Pier 11) for example. A further provider is *Eurama (Apáczai Csere János utca 12–14, Hotel Intercontinental | tel. 1 327 66 90 | www.eurama.hu)*.

You can explore Budapest by day and by night with *Absolute Walking Tours (www.absolutetours.com)*. Another option is to discover the city on a Segway Tour – the long tour lasting around 3hrs, a mini tour 90 mins. *www.citysegwaytours.com)*. *Discover Budapest Tour Center | VI, Lázár utca 16 (hinter der Oper) | tel. 1 269 38 43* Cycle tours are run by *Yellow Zebra Bike Tours (V, Sütő utca 2/Deák tér, in the courtyard | www.yellowzebrabikes.com)*. Themed tours such as a lifestyle or a baths tour are run by *Budapestbike (VII, Wesselényi utca 18, not far from the Great Synagogue, in Café Szóda | www.budapestbike.hu)*.

BUDGETING

Cappuccino	450 forints *per cup*
Lunch menu	1,800 forints *for lunch in a restaurant*
Beer	430 forints *per glass (0.5 l)*
Pick-Salami	375 forints *for 100 g salami*
Taxi	270 forints *per kilometre*
Souvenir	2,500 forints *for one bottle of Unicum herbal bitter (0.5 l)*

Boat trips: *Duna Bella/Dunai Legenda (tel. 1 2 66 41 90 | www.legenda.hu)*. You can also join Danube trips such as *Budapest by Night* and trips to the Danube Bend (pier Vigadó tér) *(www.mahart-passnave.hu)*.

CONSULATES & EMBASSIES

UK EMBASSY
Harmincad utca 6 | tel. 1 2 66 88 88| www.ukinhungary.fco.gov.uk

US EMBASSY
Szabadság tér 12| tel. 1 4 75 44 00| www.hungary.usembassy.gov

CUSTOMS

Goods for personal consumption can be imported and exported for free, e.g. 10 l spirits, 90 l wine or 800 cigarettes per person. Non-commercial quantities of items purchased or received are not subject to custom duties in Hungary but may be subject to the custom duties and import regulations of a destination country outside the EU.

EMERGENCY

Ambulance: *tel. 104* (emergency ambulance free, if an immediate medical intervention is necessary)
Police: *tel. 107,* hotline: *tel. 1 4 38 80 80*
Fire: *tel. 105*

IMMIGRATION

All you need to enter Hungary is a passport. US citizens may enter Hungary for up to 90 days for tourist or business purposes without a visa. Since Hungary joined the Schengen Area, travellers entering from another Schengen country are not subjected to regular passport inspections anymore.

INFORMATION BEFORE YOU GO

HUNGARIAN NATIONAL TOURIST OFFICE
– 46 Eaton Place | London SW1X8AL | tel. 020 78 23 04 12 | www.gotohungary.co.uk
– 447 Broadway 5th floor | Manhattan NY 10013 | tel. 212 695 12 21 | www.gotohungary.com

You will find all the basic information on *www.budapestinfo.hu*. Information and news are available on *www.budapest. com*. The Hungary guide for hotels, restaurants etc. is *www.travelport.hu*.

INFORMATION IN BUDAPEST

TOURINFORM
– www.tourinform.hu
– V, Deák Ferenc tér/Sűtő utca 2 | tel. 1 4 38 80 80 | underground 1, 2: Deák tér (117 D2) *(Ⅲ D9)*
– VI, Liszt Ferenc tér 11 | tel. 1 3 22 40 98 | underground 1: Oktogon (123 F4) *(Ⅲ E8)*

INTERNET ACCESS

Internet cafés are mainly to be found in the city centre on the Pest side of the Danube. The density is much higher near WiFi hotspots *(www.hotspotter.hu)*.

MEDIA

International daily newspapers are available from kiosks in the city centre (Vörösmarty tér, Váci utca) and in large hotels. The Budapest Times *(www.buda pesttimes.hu)* is Hungary's leading English-language source for daily news, restaurants, hotels, movies, culture and tourism. Satellite channels can be received everywhere.

MONEY & BANKS

Changing money is possible in banks, travel agencies, bureaux de change and through money-changing machines (in banks). Banks are usually open Mon–Thu 8am–4pm and Fri 8am–3pm. You will also be able to get money with the usual credit/debit cards (banks, ATMs). The currency in Hungary is the forint (Ft., HUF). Coins worth 5, 10, 20, 50 and 100 Ft are issued, as are notes worth 200, 500, 1000, 2000, 5000, 10,000 and 20,000 Ft.

OPENING HOURS & ENTRY PRICES

Unfortunately opening hours change a lot in Budapest. Hungarians have become used to suddenly standing in front of closed doors and are relaxed about it. Hardly anything has changed in recent years regarding the practice of having a very liberal attitude to the stated opening hours. Entrance fees also keep changing, but generally speaking they are quite low.

PHONE & MOBILE PHONE

Phone cards (available from post offices and newsagents) usually work with public telephones.

Phone numbers in Budapest have seven digits, the city dialling code is 1. For a local call from a landline you can omit the dialling code in Budapest. From a landline in Hungary (long distance) as well as from Hungarian mobile phones you have to dial 06 as well as the area code, i.e. for Budapest 061, followed by the phone number. The country dialling code for Hungary is 0036; if you want to call a Budapest number from a landline outside of Hungary, you have to dial 00361, then the phone number. Hungarian mobile phone numbers also

have seven digits and usually start with 20, 30 or 70. To call one, from a Hungarian landline or mobile, you always have to prefix it by 06 (e.g. 0620, then the seven-digit number). Mobile phone providers are T-Mobile *(www.t-mobile.hu)*, Pannon *(www.pannon.hu)* and Vodafone *(www.vodafone.hu)*. For guests who want to stay for an extended period or for those who come to Hungary a fair bit, it would be worthwhile purchasing a Hungarian mobile phone (e.g. from Tesco, approx. 10,000 Ft.), or at least a local SIM card for your phone if it is unlocked. To call the UK, dial 0044, to call the USA, dial 001, then the local area code minus the 0 and then the phone number.

CURRENCY CONVERTER

£	HUF	HUF	£
1	352	10	0.02
3	1,056	50	0.14
5	1,760	250	0.71
13	4,580	750	2.13
40	14,100	2,000	5.70
75	26,400	5,000	14.20
120	42,300	12,000	34.10
250	88,000	30,000	85
500	176,000	50,000	142

$	HUF	HUF	$
1	220	10	0.05
3	660	50	0.23
5	1,100	250	1.13
13	2,860	750	3.40
40	8,800	2,000	9.10
75	16,500	5,000	22.75
120	26,400	12,000	55
250	55,000	30,000	136
500	110,000	50,000	227

For current exchange rates see www.xe.com

POST

Post offices are generally open Mon–Fri 8am–6pm and Sat 8am–noon. The postage for standard letters and postcards to European countries is 210 Ft.

PUBLIC TRANSPORT

The nicest underground line, opened in 1896 and restored to its former glory in 1996, is *Földalatti* (Line 1). There are two further underground lines (Metro) – 2 and 3 (a further one is under construction) – as well as a dense network of trams, buses and trolley-buses. To get up to Castle Hill you can take the funicular *(Sikló)*, which departs from Clark Adam tér. There are commuter lines *(HÉV)* running along the northern right bank of the Danube (towards the Danube Bend) and along the southern left bank, as well as (in the east) towards Gödöllő. You can take a cog railway *(Fogaskerekűvasút)* into the hills around Budapest: it departs from Város-major on the Buda side; you can also take this railway to get to the Children's Railway *(Gyermekvasút)*.

Tickets can only be purchased before you get on the train (metro stations, machines, tobacconists); the metro stations are your best option because you can get every kind of ticket there. You will have to cancel your ticket in a machine in the train, or, if you are taking the underground, there are machines by the escalators and on the platforms. You must hold on to your ticket until you have left the station, because the inspectors usually stand at the exits.

A single ticket (320 Ft) is valid for the whole line, but if you switch lines, you must purchase a new ticket.

Because of the complicated nature of

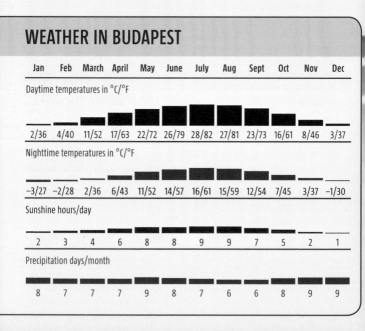

WEATHER IN BUDAPEST

	Jan	Feb	March	April	May	June	July	Aug	Sept	Oct	Nov	Dec
Daytime temperatures in °C/°F	2/36	4/40	11/52	17/63	22/72	26/79	28/82	27/81	23/73	16/61	8/46	3/37
Nighttime temperatures in °C/°F	–3/27	–2/28	2/36	6/43	11/52	14/57	16/61	15/59	12/54	7/45	3/37	–1/30
Sunshine hours/day	2	3	4	6	8	8	9	9	7	5	2	1
Precipitation days/month	8	7	7	7	9	8	7	6	6	8	9	9

the machines and the terms of carriage and because most employees working in the public transport don't speak much English, there are often difficulties. So to avoid confusion it's advisable to buy a single-day ticket or a three-day ticket (valid on all underground lines, buses, trams and the commuter trains). A day ticket (24 hrs) costs 1,550 Ft, a three-day ticket (72 hrs) 3,850 Ft. *www.bkv.hu*

Top: view from the Fisherman's Bastion

REDUCTIONS

EU citizens who are pensioners (aged 65 and older) can use Hungary's public transport (buses, trains) for free.

The *Budapest Card* (available at airports, at Tourinform, in travel agencies and hotels) gives you unlimited use of public transport and offers a wealth of further advantages and reductions. It costs 6,300 Ft (48 hrs) or 7,500 Ft (72 hrs). All reductions are listed in a brochure (*www.budapestinfo.hu*).

STREET NAMES

In 2011 Budapest's National Conservative city council decided to rename 26 squares and roads. At the time of going to press the major traffic square Moszkva tér had already become Széll Kálmán tér. Further changes will follow. There are plans to name the large Köztársaság tér near the Eastern Station after Pope John Paul II.

TAXIS

Taxis have yellow number plates and have to be fitted with a taximeter. Tariffs vary; the legal maximum is 300 Ft. basic and 240 Ft. per kilometre between 6am–10pm. *Budataxi: tel. 1 2 33 33 33 | City Taxi: tel. 1 2 11 11 11 | Főtaxi: tel. 1 2 22 22 22 | Tele 5 Taxi: tel. 1 5 55 55 55*

TICKET SALES

Ticket Express | Mon–Fri 10am–6.30pm | VI, Andrássy út 18 | tel. 30 3 03 09 99 (*) (Call centre, Mon–Fri 9am–5pm) | www. eventim.hu | underground 1: Bajcsy-Zsilinszky út (123 E5) (ꕗ D–E 8–9)

TIME

Budapest, like all of Hungary, uses Central European Time (CET) and Central European Summer Time (CEST). The changeover dates, as throughout Europe, are the last weekends in March and October.

TIPPING & SERVICE FEES

A tip of 10–15 percent is customary in restaurants. It is not the case that tips are only given voluntarily in Hungary. Restaurants are allowed to levy a service free of up to 15 percent (this does not apply to snack bars). 81 percent of that goes to the public pension fund, the rest is supposed to be divided up among the staff.

WHEN TO GO

Spring and autumn are the best times to go. During the summer months the city is often extremely crowded and gets very hot. More information under: *www. weatherinhungary.com*

USEFUL PHRASES HUNGARIAN

PRONUNCIATION

To help you say the words, we have added a simplified pronunciation guide (in square brackets). The stress is always on the first syllable of a word. Please note also:

ö   is pronounced like the 'e' in 'the'
ü   is pronounced like the 'u' in French 'tu'
gy   is pronounced like 'dy' in 'dew'
g   is pronounced as in 'go'

IN BRIEF

Yes/No/Maybe	Igen [igen]/Nem [nem]/Talán [tollaan]
Please/Thank you	Kérem [kayrem]/Köszönöm [kössönöm]
Excuse me, please!	Bocsáss meg! [botchaash meg]/Bocsásson meg, kérem! [botchaashonn meg, kayrem]
May I ...?/Pardon?	Szabad ...? [sobbodd]/Tessék? [teshshayk]
I would like to .../	Szeretnék [seretnayk]/
Have you got ...?	Van ...? [vonn]
How much is ...?	Mennyibe kerül? [mennyiber kerül]
I (don't) like that	Ez (nem) tetszik [ez (nem) tetsik]
good/bad	jó [yo]/rossz [ross]
broken/doesn't work	rossz [ross]/nem működik [nem müköddikk]
too much/much/little	túl sok [tool shokk]/sok [shokk]/kevés [kevaysh]
all/nothing	minden [minden]/semmi [shemmi]
Help!/Attention!/ Caution!	Segítség! [shegichayg]/Figyelem! [fidyelem]/Vigyázat! [vidyaazott]
ambulance/police/ fire brigade	mentő [menter]/rendőrség [rendershayg]/tűzoltóság [tüzoltoshaag]
Prohibition/forbidden	tilalom [tilollom]/tilos [tillosh]
danger/dangerous	veszély [vessay]/veszélyes [vessayesh]
May I take a photo here/ of you?	Szabad itt/Önt fényképezni? [sobod eet/önt faynye-kaypessni]

GREETINGS, FAREWELL

Good morning!/afternoon!/ evening!/night!	Jó reggelt/[yo reggelt]/napot! [yo noppot]/estét [yo eshtayt]/éjszakát! [yo ayssokkaat]
Hello!/Goodbye!	Halló! [hallo]/Viszontlátásra! [vissontlaataashro]

Beszélsz Magyarul?

"Do you speak Hungarian?" This guide will help you to say the basic words and phrases in Hungarian.

See you	Szia/Sziasztok! [sio/siosstok]
My name is ...	...-nak hívnak [...-nokk heefnokk]
What's your name?	Hogy hívják Önt? [hody heefyaak önt]/
	Hogy hívnak? [hody heefnokk]

DATE & TIME

Monday/Tuesday/	hétfő [haytföö]/kedd [ked]
Wednesday/Thursday	szerda [sairdo]/csütörtök [chüttörrtökk]
Friday/Saturday	péntek [payntek]/szombat [sombott]
Sunday/working day	vasárnap [voshaarnopp]/munkanap [munkonopp]
holiday	ünnepnap [ünnepnopp]
today/tomorrow/yesterday	ma [mo]/holnap [holnopp]/tegnap [tegnopp]
hour/minute/day/night	óra [oaro]/perc [pairts]/nap [nopp]/éjszaka [ayssokko]
What time is it?	Hány óra (van)? [haany oaro (vonn)]
It's three o'clock	Három óra (van) [haarom oaro (vonn)]
It's half past three	Fél négy (van) [fayl naydy (vonn)]
a quarter to four/	Háromnegyed négy (van) [haaromnedyed naydy
a quarter past four	(vonn)]/Negyed öt (van) [nedyed ött (vonn)]

TRAVEL

open/closed	nyitva [nyitvo]/zárva [zaarvo]
entrance/exit	bejárat [bayaarott]/kijárat [kiyaarott]
departure/arrival	indulás [indulaash]/érkezés [ayrkezaysh]
toilets/ladies/gentlemen	toalett [toallet]/hölgyek [höldyekk]/urak [urrokk]
(no) drinking water	(nem) ívóvíz [(nem) eevoveez]
Where is ...?/Where are ...?	Hol van ...? [hol vonn]/Hol vannak ...? [hol vonnokk]
left/right	balra [bollro]/jobbra [yobro]
straight ahead/back	egyenes(en) [edyenesh(en)]/vissza [visso]
close/far	közel [kerzel]/messze [messer]
bus/tram / taxi/cab	busz [buss]/villamos [vilommosh] / taxi [toxi]
U-Bahn/bus stop	metró [metro]/megálló [megalo]
parking lot/parking garage	parkoló [porrkolo]/parkolóház [porrkolohaaz]
street map/map	várostérkép [vaaroshtayrkayp]/térkép [tayrkayp]
train station	vasútállomás [voshootaalomaash]
airport	repülőtér [repülertayr]
schedule/ticket	menetrend [menetrend]/menetjegy [menetyedy]
single/return	oda [odo]/oda-vissza [odo-visso]
train/track	vonat [vonott]/vágány [vaagaany]
I would like to rent ...	...-t szeretnék bérelni [seretnayk bayrelni]
a car/a bicycle	autót [owto]/biciklit [bitsiklit]

petrol/gas station	benzinkút [benzeenkoot]
petrol/gas / diesel	benzin [benzeen]/gázolaj [gaazoloy]
breakdown/repair shop	defekt [defekt]/műhely [mühay]

FOOD & DRINK

Could you please book a table for tonight for four?	Foglaljon kérem nekünk ma estére egy asztalt négy személyre [foglalyon kayrem nekünk mo eshtayrer edy osstollt naydy semayrer]
The menu, please	Az étlapot kérem [os aytlopot kayrem]
Could I please have ...?	Hozna nekem kérem ...? [hosno nekem kayrem]
salt/pepper/sugar/vinegar	só [sho]/bors [borsh]/cukor [tsukor]/ecet [etset]
milk/cream/lemon/oil	tej [tay]/tejszín [tayseen]/citrom [tsitrom]/olaj [oloy]
with/without ice/ sparkling	jéggel [yaygel]/jég nélkül [yayg naykül]/szénsavas [saynshovosh]/szénsavmentes [saynnshan-mentesh]
vegetarian/allergy	vegetáriánus [vegetaariaanush]/allergia [olairgio]
May I have the bill, please?	Fizetni szeretnék, kérem [fizzetni seretnayk, kayrem]
bill/receipt	számla [saamlo]/nyugta [nyoogto]

SHOPPING

I'd like .../I'm looking for ...	Szeretnék ... [seretnayk]/Keresek ... [keresek]
pharmacy/chemist	gyógyszertár [dyodyssairtaar]/drogéria [drogayrio]
baker/market/kiosk	pékség [paykshayg]/piac [piots]/trafik [trofik]
100 grammes/1 kilo	száz gramm [saas grom]/egy kiló [edy kilo]
expensive/cheap/price	drága [draago]/olcsó [olcho]/ár [aar]
more/less	több [töb]/kevesebb [kevvesheb]

ACCOMMODATION

I have booked a room	Szobát rendeltem [sobaat rendeltem]
Do you have any ... left?	Van még szabad ...? [vonn mayg sobod]
single room	egyágyas szobájuk [eddyaadyosh sobaayukk]
double room	kétágyas szobájuk [kaytaadyosh sobaayukk]
breakfast/half board	reggeli [reggeli]/félpanzió [faylponsioan]
full board (American plan)/ Balkon	teljes panzió [telyesh ponsioan]/ erkély [airkay]
shower/sit-down bath	tusoló [toosholo]/fürdőszoba [fürdösobo]
key/room card	kulcs [kultch]/szobakártya [sobokaartyo]
luggage/suitcase	csomag [chomogg]/bőrönd [börönnd]

BANKS, MONEY & CREDIT CARDS

bank/ATM	bank [bonk]/bankautomata [bonkowtomaato]
pin code	titkos kód [titkosh koad]
I'd like to change ...	Szeretnék ... váltani [seretnayk ... vaaltoni]

cash/credit card	készpénz [kayspaynz]/hitelkártya [hitelkartyo]
bill/coin	bankjegy [bonkyedy]/fémpénz [faympaynz]
change	aprópénz [opropaynz]

HEALTH

doctor/dentist/ paediatrician	orvos [orvosh]/fogorvos [fogorvos]/ gyerekorvos [dyerekorvos]
hospital/ emergency clinic	kórház [koarhaas]/ sürgősségi rendelés [shürgöshshaygi rendelaysh]
fever/pain	láz [laaz]/fájdalom [foydollom]
diarrhoea/nausea	hasmenés [hoshmanaysh]/rosszullét [rossulayt]
pain reliever/ tablet	fájdalomcsillapító [foydollomchilopeeto]/ tabletta [tobletto]

POST, TELECOMMUNICATIONS & MEDIA

stamp/letter/postcard	bélyeg [bayeg]/levél [levayl]/képeslap [kaypeshlopp]
I need a landline phone card	Szükségem van telefonkártyára vezetékes telefonhoz [sükshaygem vonn telefonkartyaaro vesetaykesh telefonhoz]
I'm looking for a prepaid card for my mobile	Feltöltős telefonkártyát keresek a mobil-telefonomhoz [feltöltösh telefonkartyaat keresek o mobiltelefonomhoz]
internet access	internethozzáférés [internethossaafayraysh]

NUMBERS

0	nulla [nullo]	18	tizennyolc [tizzennyolts]
1	egy [edy]	19	tizenkilenc [tizzenkilents]
2	kettő/két [kettö/kayt]	20	húsz [hooss]
3	három [haarom]	21	huszonegy [hussonedy]
4	négy [naydy]	30	harminc [horrmints]
5	öt [öt]	40	negyven [nedyven]
6	hat [hott]	50	ötven [ötven]
7	hét [hayt]	60	hatvan [hottvonn]
8	nyolc [nyolts]	70	hetven [hetven]
9	kilenc [kilents]	80	nyolcvan [nyoltsvonn]
10	tíz [teess]	90	kilencven [kilentsven]
11	tizenegy [tizzenedy]	100	száz [saas]
12	tizenkettő/tizenkét [tizenketter/tizenkayt]	200	kétszáz [kaytsaas]
13	tizenhárom [tizzenhaarom]	1000	ezer [ezzer]
14	tizennégy [tizzennaydy]	2000	kétezer [kaytezzer]
15	tizenöt [tizzenöt]	10000	tízezer [teezzezzer]
16	tizenhat [tizzenhott]	½	fél [fayl]
17	tizenhét [tizzenhayt]	¼	(egy) negyed [(edy) nedyed]

NOTES

FOR YOUR NEXT HOLIDAY ...

MARCO POLO TRAVEL GUIDES

MARCO POLO

With ROAD ATLAS & PULL-OUT MAP

LAKE GARDA

BALDO WITH MOUNTAIN BIKE
ia Malcesine takes bikes too

OSES "IN SALÒ
colate "Bacetti"

Insider Tips

MARCO POLO

With STREET ATLAS & PULL-OUT MAP

NEW YORK

OWS, WILD FLOWERS AND SKYSCRAPERS
chic: the High Line in Chelsea

AL ON CLOUD NINE
tap bar at 230 Fifth Street

Insider Tips

MARCO POLO

With ROAD ATLAS & PULL-OUT MAP

FRENCH RIVIERA
NICE, CANNES & MONACO

SPECTACULAR GRAND CANYON DU VERDON
Breath-taking scenery that takes some beating

SNIFFING THE AIR
The perfume manufacturers of Grasse

Insider Tips

www.marcopolouk.com

MARCO POLO

With ROAD ATLAS & PULL-OUT MAP

ALLORCA

AN FLAIR IN THE MEDITERRANEAN
Mallorca's most beautiful beach

E "IN" CROWD MEET
Fonda in Deià

Insider Tips

MARCO POLO

With STREET ATLAS & PULL-OUT MAP

BERLIN

A STUNNING ISLAND JUST FOR ART
Showcasing treasures from around the world

STAY COOL AT NIGHT
scene sets the trend

Insider Tips

PACKED WITH INSIDER TIPS
BEST WALKS AND TOURS
FULL-COLOUR PULL-OUT MAP
AND STREET ATLAS

www.marcopolouk.com

STREET ATLAS

The green line   indicates the Walking tours (p. 90-95)

All tours are also marked on the pull-out map

Photo: Vajdahunyad Castle

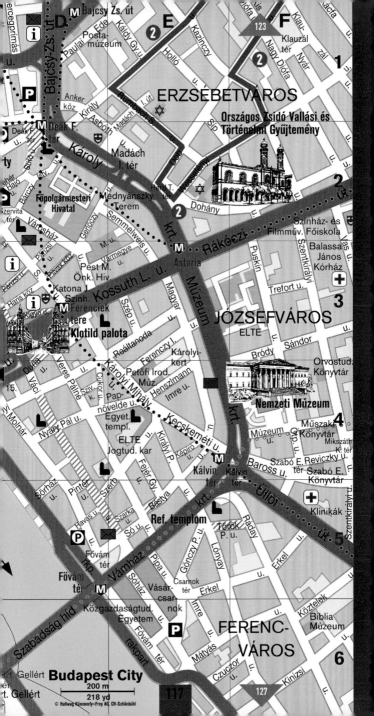

ERZSÉBETVÁROS

Országos Zsidó Vallási és
Történelmi Gyűjtemény

Bajcsy Zs. út

Posta-
múzeum

Anker
köz

Deák F.
tér

Károly

Madách
l. tér

Főpolgármesteri
Hivatal

Mednyánszky
Terem

Dohány

Színház- és
Filmműv. Főiskola

Balassa
János
Kórház

Városház

Pest M.
Önk. Hiv.

Katona J.
Szính.

Ferenciek
tere

Klotild palota

Astoria

Kossuth L. u.

Rákóczi

Trefort u.

JÓZSEFVÁROS

ELTE

Bródy   Sándor

Orvostud.
Könyvtár

Reáltanoda

Ferenczy l.

Petőfi Irod.
Múz

Papnövelde u.

Egyet.
templ.

ELTE
Jogtud. kar

Károlyi
kert

Henszlmann
Imre u.

Károlyi Mihály

Kecskeméti u.

Kálvin
tér

Kálvin
tér

Nemzeti Múzeum

Műszaki
Könyvtár

Baross u.

Szabó E.
tér

Szabó E.
Könyvtár

Ref. templom

Török
P. u.

Klinikák

Szabadság híd

Fővám
tér

Vámház

Közgazdaságtud.
Egyetem

Vásár-
csar-
nok

FERENC-
VÁROS

Biblia
Múzeum

Gellért

Budapest City

200 m
218 yd

© Hallwag Kümmerly+Frey AG, CH-Schönbühl

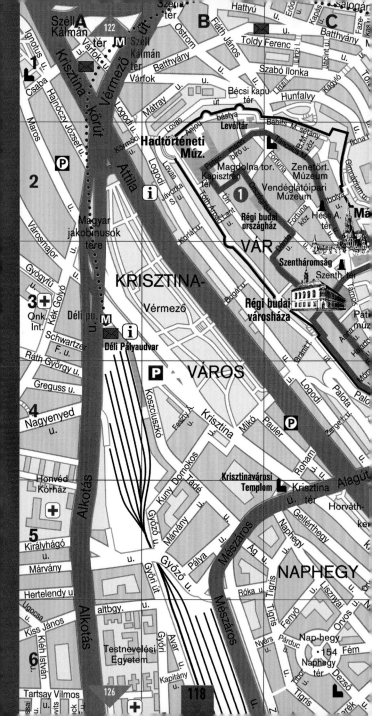

A

Szél Kálmán tér
Ignotus u.
Csaba u.
Maros u.
1

P
Hajnóczy József u.
Krisztina körút
2
Vérmező út
Városmajor u.
Gyógyfű u.
Kék Golyó
3 ✚
Onk.
Int.
Schwartzer F. u.
Ráth György u.
Greguss u.
4
Nagyenyed u.
Honvéd Kórház
5 ✚
Királyhágó u.
Márvány
Hertelendy u.
Ugocsa
Kiss János
Kléh István u.
6
Tartsay Vilmos

B

Széll Kálmán tér
M Várfok u.
Széll Kálmán tér
Várfok u.
Logodi u.
Batthyány u.
Mátray u.
Lovas
Kőrmöci u.
Attila u.
Logodi u.
Lovas út
Jávorka S u.
i
Magyar jakobinusok tere
KRISZTINA-
Vérmező
Logodi u.
M Déli pu.
P ✉ **i**
Déli Pályaudvar
P
VÁROS
Kosciuszkó
Feszty Á.
Krisztina u.
Mikó Pauler
P
Kuny Domokos
Tadé
Győző u.
Márvány
Pálya u.
Avar
Győri u.
altbgy.
Győző u.
Testnevelési Egyetem
Kapitány u.
126
118

Ostrom u.
Batthyány u.
Várfok u.
Bécsi kapu tér
bástya
Lovas
Anjou
Kard u.
Hadtörténeti Múz.
biró u.
Petermann
bíró u.
Levéltár
Kapisztrán tér
Magdolna tor.
Tóth Árpád sétány
Úri u.
Tárnok
1
Régi budai országház
VÁR
Szentháromság
Bugát u.
Régi budai városháza
Logodi u.
Krisztina u.
Roham u.
Zerge lépcső u.
Krisztinavárosi Templom ⌐ Krisztina tér
Horváth-kert
Gellérthegy
Naphegy
Naphegy u.
Aq. u.
Mészáros u.
Róka u.
Tigris u.
Fenyő u.
Nyers u.
Párduc u.
Mészáros u.
Győző u.
NAPHEGY
Lisznyai u.
Nap-hegy
•154 Fém
Naphegy tér ⌐
Orvos u.
Dezső u.
Tigris u.

C

Salgótar...
Hattyú u.
Fiáth János u.
Toldy Ferenc Batthyány u.
Jácint u.
Szabó Ilonka u.
Hunfalvy u.
Szentháromság u.
Babits M. sétány
B.M. köz
Bástya köz
Fortuna u.
Zenetört. Múzeum
Vendéglátóipari Múzeum
Fortuna köz
Hess A. tér
Gimnázium u.
Szenth. tér
Táncsics
Pati múz
Anna u.
Hattyú köz
Móra u.
Palota út
Palo...
Alagút
Alagút

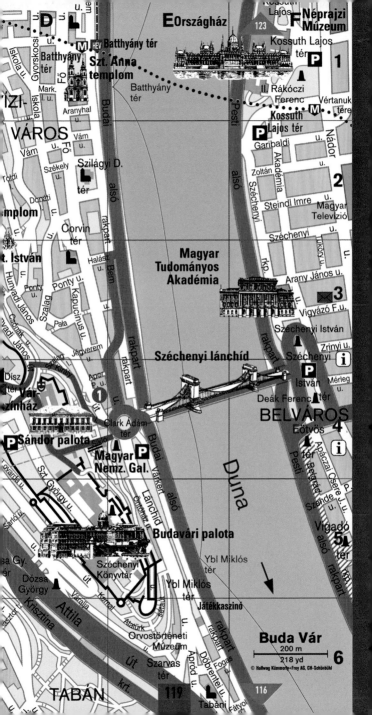

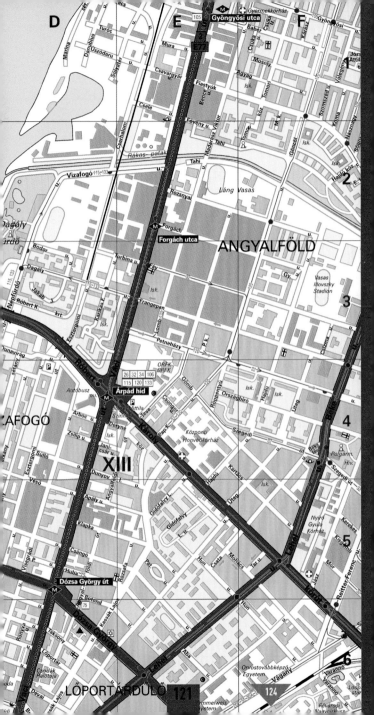

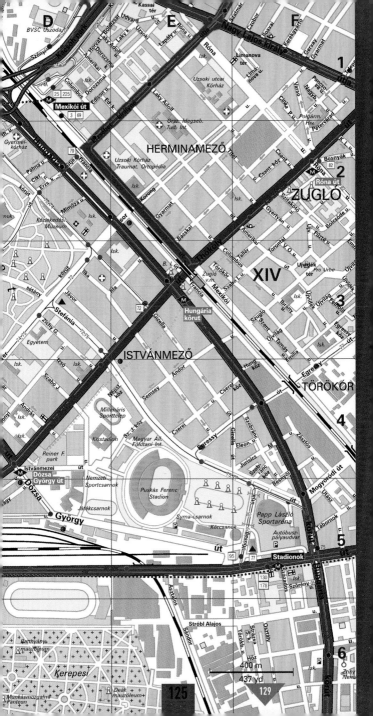

D Kerepesi **E** **F**

125

Munkásmozgalmi
Panteon

Deák
mauzóleum

temető
Kossuth
mauzóleum

Iosk.

Zrínyi
Nemz.

Tisztes

Ciprus

Gyökénce

BKV-Előre
sporttelep

Sport

MTK Hidegkúti
Stadion

Salgótarjáni

1

37-37A

Salgótarjáni

83

Köbánya

Szemafor
Loko tér

Vagon

2

óbánc

Visi Imre u.

Samuel

Golgota
tér

Sárkány u.

Vajda Péter

Golgota
u.

KEREPESDŰLŐ

Bíró Lajos

Szabadság
park

3

Lengyel
sétány

Lengyel
légiósok

rczy-
kert

Rozsa

Reguly Antal

Isk.

Benyovszky Móric

TISZTVISELŐ-

Elnök

TELEP

Centenárium park

Örcy

Batsányi u.

Egyetem

Nagyvárad tér

Rezső
tér

Nagyvárad
tér

Delej

Rezső u.

Isk.

Pedagógiai
Múzeum

Györffy I.

Vajda János

Villám

Tinódi

Ország-
park
Planetárium

sétány

4

Mutatványos
tér

Istváp

Gyali

Gyáli

Batthyány Ottó

103

254E

Ifjúsági

FTC Stadion

Népliget

Szent László
Kórház

Nemzetközi
autóbusz
pályaudvar

Jurta színház

Ivanka u.

Gyáli u.

ZMNE
Bólyai János
Katonai Műszaki
Főisk. Kar

Üllői

5

Ecseri út

Siketec

Könyves Kálmán

Lenkey u.

Gyáli u.

Péceli

Egyetem

Ecseri

Epreserdő u.

Ifjumunk

erencvárosi
pályaudvar

IX

Péceli

Szerkocsi

Vaskocsi

Szekereny köz

Gyáli

Sörivény u.

Vasktér u.

Tölés u.

129

Isk.

Isk.

6

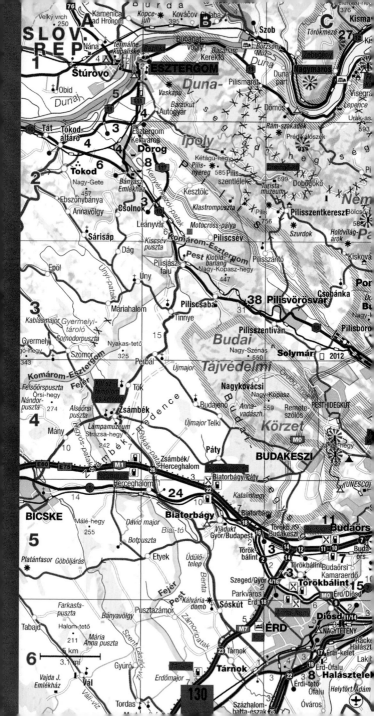

KEY TO STREET ATLAS

Autópálya / Autobahn		Motorway / Autoroute
Négysávos út / Vierspurige Straße		Road with four lanes / Route à quatre voies
Átmenő út / Durchgangsstraße		Thoroughfare / Route de transit
Főútvonal / Hauptstraße		Main road / Route principale
Egyéb út / Sonstige Straßen		Other roads / Autres routes
Információ - Parkolóhely / Information - Parkplatz	**i** **P**	Information - Parking place / Information - Parking
Hajókikötő - Hajóútvonal / Anlegestelle - Schifffahrtslinie		Landing place - Shipping route / Embarcadère - Ligne de navigation
Egyirányú utca - Sétálóutca / Einbahnstraße - Fußgängerzone		One-way street - Pedestrian zone / Rue à sens unique - Zone piétonne
Fővasútvonal állomással / Hauptbahn mit Bahnhof		Main railway with station / Chemin de fer principal avec gare
Egyéb vasútvonal / Sonstige Bahn		Other railway / Autre ligne
Kötélpálya / Standseilbahn		Cableway / Funiculaire
Földalatti vasút / U-Bahn	• • • **M** • • • •	Underground / Métro
Villamos - Gyorsjárat / Straßenbahn - Schnellbuslinie	●—4—● 13	Tramway - Express bus-route / Tramway - Ligne d'autobus à service rapide
Autóbuszvonal - Trolibuszvonal / Buslinie - O-Buslinie	●—24—● 75	Bus-route - Trolleybus-route / Ligne d'autobus - Ligne de trolleybus
Templom - Látványos templom / Kirche - Sehenswerte Kirche		Church - Church of interest / Église - Église remarquable
Zsinagóga - Kápolna / Synagoge - Kapelle		Synagogue - Chapel / Synagogue - Chapelle
Postahivatal / Postamt		Post office / Bureau de poste
Rendőrség - Emlékmű / Polizeistation - Denkmal	● Å	Police station - Monument / Poste de police - Monument
Kórház - Ifjúsági szálló / Krankenhaus - Jugendherberge	✛ ▲	Hospital - Youth hostel / Hôpital - Auberge de jeunesse
Beépítés - Középületek / Bebauung - Öffentliches Gebäude		Built-up area - Public building / Zone bâtie - Bâtiment public
Iparvidék - Park, erdő / Industriegelände - Park, Wald		Industrial area - Park, forest / Zone industrielle - Parc, bois
Város menti sétálás / Stadtspaziergänge		Walking tours / Promenades en ville
MARCO POLO Highlight	★	MARCO POLO Highlight

INDEX

The index contains all of the attractions and museums in Budapest and all of the destinations described in this travel guide. Bold figures refer to the main entry.

CREDITS

WRITE TO US

e-mail: info@marcopologuides.co.uk

Did you have a great holiday? Is there something on your mind? Whatever it is, let us know! Whether you want to praise, alert us to errors or give us a personal tip – MARCO POLO would be pleased to hear from you. We do everything we can to provide the very latest information for your trip.

Nevertheless, despite all of our authors' thorough research, errors can creep in. MARCO POLO does not accept any liability for this. Please contact us by e-mail or post.

MARCO POLO Travel Publishing Ltd Pinewood, Chineham Business Park Crockford Lane, Chineham Basingstoke, Hampshire RG24 8AL United Kingdom

PICTURE CREDITS
Cover Photograph: Parliament and Chain Bridge (Look: age fotostock)
Images: DuMont Bildarchiv: Freyer (24 top); DuMont Bildarchiv: Kalmár (96); R. Freyer (flap r., 2 centre top, 6, 7, 15, 21, 22, 30, 41, 49, 52, 70, 73, 84, 96/97, 98/99, 102 top, 109); Hotel Central Basilica (88); Huber: Pignatelli (94); © iStockphoto.com: benoit faure (17 bottom); Fanni Király: Varga Gábor György (16 bottom); K-Labor: Katalin Karsay (16 centre); Laif: Barth (4), Galli (79), Gerald (58), Hahn (2 top, 5, 9, 18/19, 25, 76, 87, 93, 99), Modrow (62 r.), Steinhilber (8), Stukhard (80); Terra Magica: Lenz (33, 62 l., 63, 102 bottom); H. Leue (2 bottom, 3 top, 38, 56/57, 61, 66/67, 103); Look: age fotostock (1 top, 46, 55), Fleisher (42, 50), Pompe (45, 65, 68, 97, 98), TerraVista (10/11); mauritius images: age (24 bottom), Alamy (48), Blume Bild (34), Flüeler (92), World Picture (flap r.); Johannes Schuler (17 top); T. Stankiewicz (2 centre bottom, 3 centre, 3 bottom, 12, 26/27, 37, 74/75, 82/83, 90/91); R. Stiens (1 bottom); Trafó: Katalin Karsay (16 top)

1st Edition 2012
Worldwide Distribution: Marco Polo Travel Publishing Ltd, Pinewood, Chineham Business Park, Crockford Lane, Basingstoke, Hampshire RG24 8AL, United Kingdom. Email: sales@marcopolouk.com
© MAIRDUMONT GmbH & Co. KG, Ostfildern
Chief editor: Michaela Lienemann (concept, managing editor), Marion Zorn (concept, text editor)
Author: Rita Stiens; Editor: Corinna Walkenhorst
Programme supervision: Ann-Katrin Kutzner, Nikolai Michaelis, Silwen Randebrock
Picture editor: Barbara Schmid, Gabriele Forst
What's hot: wunder media, Munich;
Cartography street atlas: © MAIRDUMONT, Ostfildern; Hallwag Kümmerly+Frey AG, CH-Schönbühl/Bern;
Cartography pull-out map: © MAIRDUMONT, Ostfildern
Design: milchhof: atelier, Berlin; Front cover, pull-out map cover, page 1: factor product munich
Translated from German by Michael Scuffil, Leverkusen; editor of the English edition: Tony Halliday, Oxford
Phrase book in cooperation with Ernst Klett Sprachen GmbH, Stuttgart, Editorial by Pons Wörterbücher

DOS & DON'TS

These things are best avoided in Budapest

ORDERING WITHOUT CHECKING PRICES FIRST

Unfortunately, waiters often tend to make very expensive recommendations. In addition, the prices for open wines are not for a glass, but only for 1 cl. The bill will then say a higher price because the glass of wine served contained more than 1 cl. For that reason it is important not to order anything without having checked on the menu what the recommended wine or dish really costs.

CHANGING MONEY ON THE STREET

Always avoid changing money on the street. The danger of being scammed is very high. They will count the money in front of you, but you will somehow end up with fewer notes in your hand than you were told you would be given.

FALLING FOR FAKE POLICE OFFICERS

It doesn't happen very often, but you could encounter someone posing as a police officer. There is only one thing to remember: police officers are allowed to check your papers on the street, but not your wallet!

LEAVING YOUR CAR UNGUARDED

The risk of theft is much greater if you do not have an electronic immobilizer and alarm. If you come in your own car,

you should park it in a secure car park for the duration of your stay.

MISLEADING EXCHANGE RATES

If you're changing money anywhere other than a bank, you should check whether the exchange rate being advertised is actually the one being paid out. Customers are often lured in by favourable exchange rates, but it's often the case that these only apply to large transactions (such as $1,000). That's why it is safer to ask first whether the advertised rate also applies to the sum you wish to change.

FALLING FOR INCORRECT NOTE

It is advisable to check every note closely and, if you are paying with a large denomination, to leave it on the table until the change has been paid out.

INVITING CHANCE ACQUAINTANCES

You should check prices if you want to invite a lady you have only just met. It could be that such women are working as decoys and you end up getting an astronomical bill in the restaurant. The menu often won't list the price, or at least not clearly, but you'll still not be allowed to leave until you have paid up.